Midget Submarines
of the Second World War

The British *X-Craft* were the most successful midget submarines of the Second World War. This photograph shows *XT1*, belonging to the *XT* training craft series, moving away from her depot ship in Holy Loch in February 1944. The *XT* series had a number of differences from the *X* and *XE* series of operational craft. The 'cargo' was a inert weight which could not be released: no night periscope was fitted and the induction mast was a fixed structure which could not be lowered. (Imperial War Museum: A21692)

Midget Submarines
of the Second World War

Paul Kemp

Plans and drawings by David J Hill

CAXTON EDITIONS

First published in Great Britain in 1999 by Chatham Publishing,
61 Frith Street, London W1V 5TA

Chatham Publishing is an imprint of Gerald Duckworth & Co Ltd

This edition published 2003 by Caxton Editions
an imprint of The Caxton Publishing Group

British Library Cataloguing in Publication Data
A catalogue record for this book is available from the
British Library

ISBN 1 84067 521 7

Plans and drawings by David J Hill

Designed and typeset by Tony Hart, Isle of Wight

Printed and bound in Dubai

Contents

Acknowledgements

I am deeply grateful to the following for their help in the preparation of this book: Commander Thomas Belke USN; Harvey Bennette; Admiral Gino Birindelli; Dick Boyle, officer-in-charge of the United States Navy's only midget submarine, the ill-fated *X-1*; Commander Richard Compton-Hall MBE RN, former Director of the Royal Navy Submarine Museum; Debbie Corner, Keeper of Photographs at the Royal Navy Submarine Museum; Colin Bruce and Allison Duffield of the Department of Printed Books at the Imperial War Museum; Ed Finney of the US Navy Historical Service; *Oberfahnrich z.S (ad)* Klaus Goetsch; Frank Goldsworthy; Eric Grove; Lieutenant Commander George Honour DSC RNVR; Peter Jung of the *Kriegsarchiv* in Vienna; Klaus Matthes; Jane Middleton for her excellent and imaginative drawings; Dott. Achille Rastelli; Captain Richard Sharpe OBE RN, Editor of *Jane's Fighting Ships*; Marco Spertini; Commander J J Tall MBE RN, Director of the Royal Navy Submarine Museum; David Taylor; Captain A V Walker DSC RN; the late Commander H P Westmacott DSO DSC RN. Special thanks are due to David Hill for the line drawings. The authorities of the Democratic People's Republic of Korea and of the Islamic Republic of Iran still feel unable to answer any of my requests for information on the midget submarines in their service.

This book is respectfully dedicated to the memory of my friend Gus Britton (1922-97) of the Royal Navy's Submarine Museum. He taught me more about submarine history than I care to remember. His comments – both constructive and profane – on my many manuscripts were always perceptive and enlightening. He is greatly missed.

Paul Kemp,
Maidstone, January 1999

Abbreviations

ASW. anti-submarine warfare

bhp. brake horsepower

ERA. Engine Room Artificer

GIUK. Greenland-Iceland-United Kingdom
GRT. Gross Registered Tonnage

HMS. His Majesty's Ship
HMS/M. His Majesty's Submarine
hp. horsepower

IJN. Imperial Japanese Navy
in. inch(es)

kc/s. kilocycles
kg. kilogrammes
km. kilometres
kt(s). knot(s)
KW. kilowatts

lbs. pounds
LCF. Landing Craft Flak
LCG. Landing Craft Gun
LCS. Landing Craft Support

m. metres
MTB. Motor torpedo-boat

nm. nautical miles

oa. overall

RANVR. Royal Australian Navy Volunteer Reserve
RN. Royal Navy
RNR. Royal Naval Reserve
RNVR. Royal Naval Volunteer Reserve
rpm. revolutions per minute

SANVR. South African Navy Volunteer Reserve
SDV. Swimmer Delivery Vehicle
SEAL. Sea-Air-Land (Team). US Navy Special Forces
SIS. Secret Intelligence Service
SOE. Special Operations Executive
SSBN. Nuclear-powered ballistic missile submarine
STV. *Sottotenente di Vascello* (Sub-Lieutenant in Italian Navy)

t/m³. Tons per cubic metre
TV. *Tenente di Vascello* (2nd Lieutenant in Italian Navy)

USN. United States Navy
USS. United States Ship

Introduction

THE MIDGET SUBMARINE is one of the most potent weapons of war developed in the twentieth century. Yet it is an extremely old form of naval warfare with the first, although unsuccessful, attack being launched in 1776. In the early days of submarine warfare this century, all submarines were *midget* craft. But as the submarine grew, there arose a requirement for small craft which could penetrate a defended harbour and attack shipping. This single requirement has since been expanded to include a host of other roles. Experience with the midget submarine showed that these small craft could accomplish operations of considerable strategic importance with effects out of all proportion to their small size.

During the Second World War all the major belligerent navies with the exception of the United States, France and the USSR employed midget submarines or specially trained assault frogmen. The absence of France from this field is easily explained – the capitulation of France in June 1940 effectively removed them from the war, while the United States possessed conventional forces in abundance and thus did not need to resort to this form of warfare. However, the absence of the Soviet Union from this area of operations is puzzling given the pioneering work done by Russian engineers in submarine development. But the highly individualistic nature of midget submarine operations may not have been one that sat easily alongside the centralised Soviet command structure.

Three kinds of midget submarine made their appearance during the Second World War: human torpedoes (the Italian *Maiale* and British Chariot); small submersibles (the German *Neger* and associated craft and the Japanese *Kaiten*) and true midget submarines (the Japanese *Ko-Hyoteki*, the Italian CA/CB types, the British *X-Craft* and the German *Seehund*). These craft can also be further divided into the practical and therefore successful (British *X-Craft*, Italian *Maiale*), those that were enthusiastically designed but impractical (British Chariot, Japanese *Ko-Hyoteki*, German *Biber*) and the suicidal either by accident or design (British *Welman*, German *Neger*, Japanese *Kaiten* and its various derivatives). Researching material on these craft is not easy. In many cases their design and construction was carried out in such speed and secrecy that no proper written records of trials and performance were made.

Each of the various belligerents had different reasons for entering the field of midget submarine/submersible development. Italy and Britain used the weapons for offensive purposes – to attack targets which were beyond the reach of more conventional weapons. Japan began by designing midget submarines for an offensive role, but as their strategy changed so did the role of their midget submarines change to a defensive one. German midgets and submersibles were designed for wholly defensive role.

Italy

It was the Italians who took the lead in developing this new form of naval warfare. In 1915 Italy had abandoned her commitments to her Austrian and German partners and had joined the Entente, largely on the grounds that an Anglo-French victory would satisfy Italian territorial claims against Austria. The Italian Navy was slightly larger (and was considerably larger when bolstered by Anglo-French forces) than the *Kuk Kriegsmarine* across the Adriatic. But neither side was prepared to risk upsetting the balance of power by exposing their Dreadnought battleships in a fleet engagement, adopting instead a passive strategy, glaring at each other from the behind the nets, coastal batteries and minefields of their respective ports of Taranto and Pola. Therefore the Italians seized on the

A replica of Ezra Lee's famous *Turtle*, which became the inspiration for many subsequent designs as well as hinting at many of the problems. (Author)

submersible/midget submarine as a means of attacking the Austrian fleet without risking any of their capital ships in the process. The Italian talent for this sort of warfare was amply demonstrated in 1918 and carried on in the inter-war period. Here Italy faced a strategic situation where she was 'sandwiched' by the combined British and French fleets in the western Mediterranean and by the British fleet in the eastern Mediterranean. It was Italy's military adventure in Abyssinia in 1935 which led to the establishment of a unit, eventually known as the *Decima Mas*, dedicated to these operations. The war in Abyssinia brought down a good deal of international opprobrium on the Italian government and the situation was very tense. To reduce the odds against the *Regia Marina* a weapon was required which could be cheaply built for attacks on naval targets in harbour.

Why was the *Decima Mas* such an efficient unit when, it must be admitted, the Italian forces declined in efficiency as the war progressed and turned against them? Armchair naval historians who delight in writing off the wartime operations of the *Regia Marina* would do well to remember that in under three years of warfare, *Decima Mas* was responsible for sinking or damaging four warships and twenty-seven merchant ships totalling 265,352 tons in operations ranging from Alexandria to Gibraltar. At the end of the war *Decima Mas* was poised to strike as far afield as New York. No better proof of how the unit was regarded by the Allies can be found than in the story of a young *Decima Mas* officer who had been captured by the British at Gibraltar. He subsequently developed TB and was selected by the Red Cross for repatriation to Italy on compassionate grounds. The officer was literally one step away from the repatriation ship when he was whisked away and packed off to a POW camp in the United States. The Admiralty had belatedly discovered his name on the list and were not prepared to let him go on account of his potential usefulness to the Italian cause in training human torpedo operators or in directing operations himself.[1]

Firstly, and it is not easy to quantify, their remarkable efficiency came from something in the Latin temperament. The Italians lacked nothing when it came to displaying individual courage and were glad and willing to volunteer for hazardous duty where a man's individual prowess could stand out. They were not, on the other hand, so happy about playing a small part in a large organisation. Secondly, *Decima Mas* was remarkably free from the class distinctions which bedevilled the Italian armed forces, where officers enjoyed exceptional privileges – even in submarines the wardroom had a separate galley. Things were very different in the *Decima Mas* where officers and men enjoyed a close relationship. Paradoxically many of the officers in *Decima Mas* came from the nobility while many of their men were from comparatively humble

backgrounds. Loyalty both upwards and downwards was absolute. Thirdly, *Decima Mas* was not prey to the logistic problems which were endemic in the Italian military establishment. This was in no small measure due to royal patronage, the unit being commanded by the Duke of Aosta, a cousin of the King, who used his influence ruthlessly and shamelessly to procure the unprocurable. However, the reverse of this particular coin was that *Decima Mas* was run very much as a private fiefdom within the *Regia Marina* and the possibility of using its talents to deliver a decisive blow in concert with more conventional forces was not exploited as effectively as it might have been.[2]

Great Britain

Britain was the least likely country to take an interest in midget submarines of any kind. Even though the Royal Navy was numerically smaller than it had been at the apogee of its greatness in 1914, Britain was still the pre-eminent maritime power, with battlefleets deployed in the Atlantic and Mediterranean and smaller squadrons in other areas of the world. The midget submarine was the weapon of the weaker power, designed for covert attacks on targets such as the capital ships which, even in 1939, were regarded as the *ne plus ultra* of naval power. Britain had more to fear from the operations of these craft than she had to gain by developing them herself.

However, the German occupation of Norway in 1940 presented the Royal Navy with a new and perplexing situation. From February 1942 the *Kriegsmarine* maintained a powerful surface task force in various Norwegian fjords centred around the 42,000-ton battleship *Tirpitz*. Though this force hardly ever put to sea it exercised a considerable influence on the conduct of British maritime operations. The German ships were placed to break out into the Atlantic and posed a continual threat to the convoys taking supplies to the Soviet ports of Murmansk and Archangel.[3] Their mere presence in their Norwegian lairs was sufficient to force a worried Admiralty to maintain superior numbers of British ships in home waters when they could have been more profitably employed elsewhere. In short a significant proportion of the Royal Navy was employed in guarding against a threat which never materialised. Moreover, the German ships were relatively safe in the Norwegian anchorages: they could not be assaulted by conventional ships and submarines stood no chance of penetrating the fjords. Until the development of precision high-level bombing by the RAF, air power likewise stood no chance of sinking these ships. They appeared invulnerable. Thus in much the same way as the Italians had seized on midget submarines/submersibles in the First World War, so did Britain in the Second. An added push in that direction was given by the activities of the Italian *Decima Mas* in the

Mediterranean and thus Britain, the strongest naval power in the world, was forced to adopt the traditional weapon of the weaker power.

However, in contrast to Italian (and German) practice, British midget submarine and submersible operators were always part of the Royal Navy. The 12th and 14th Submarine Flotillas were properly constituted units of the fleet. This brought important benefits. It was a positive synthesis of the enthusiasm and dedication of the RNR and RNVR officers who volunteered for these hazardous operations with the professional skills of the RN officer. It also kept midget submarine and submersible operators in touch with the mainstream navy and navy support organisations such as the Royal Corps of Naval Constructors and allowed officers from the 'regular' navy to have an input into midget submarine operations. The one occasion in British practice when a underwater assault craft – the *Welman* – was conceived and built in isolation was little short of disastrous.

Japan

On the other side of the world, the Imperial Japanese Navy (IJN) had been pursuing the development of midget submarines since the end of the First World War, which had shattered the cosy relationship which Japan had hitherto enjoyed with the west. Moreover, at the 1922 Washington Naval Conference, Japan was forced to accept a quantitative discrepancy between her forces and those of Britain and the United States. The Naval Staff seized upon the midget submarine as one means whereby the imbalance could be rectified. The Japanese thought of war with the United States in terms of a climactic action between their two battlefleets – a battle on the same lines as Tsushima and Jutland. In this context midget submarines would be used to whittle down the American advantage before the two fleets met. For this purpose they could be carried to the operational area in special vessels and used as opportunity allowed. It followed that their success depended on the enemy being unaware of their deployment and thus secrecy was essential at all stages of their design, construction and deployment.

The Washington Naval Treaty of 1922 and the London Naval Treaty of 1930 imposed quantitative limits of the size of the IJN relative to the British and American Navies: 60 per cent of capital ship, aircraft carrier and cruiser tonnage and 70 per cent of light cruiser and destroyer tonnage. However, the Japanese were allowed parity in submarine tonnage. There were many in Japan who resented this state of affairs and as Japan's policy in China throughout the 1920s and 1930s led to a cooling in relations with Britain and the United States, there were those who considered how this situation could be circumvented. The construction of ships which covertly breached treaty limits was one solution as was the policy of building ships with maximum offensive power on minimum displacement. The development of naval air power, which was not covered by the disarmament treaties, was a third option and a fourth was the adoption of unique tactics and weapons allied to rigorous training in manoeuvres.

Japanese plans for fighting the Americans envisaged the US Navy coming across the Pacific to fight a decisive action with the Japanese fleet in its home waters. Since the Americans possessed a superior number of ships, the Japanese planned a series of attritional engagements using surface and submarine torpedo attacks to reduce the numbers slightly. They then planned to intercept the Americans in an area to the west of the Ogasawara Islands and destroy them in a climactic gunnery duel. In the night before this great battle, the Americans would be subjected to yet more torpedo attacks to shift the balance still further in favour of the Japanese and disrupt the American formation. There were two products of this strategy. The first was improved torpedoes, capable of being fired at great ranges, the best known of which is the Type 93 'Long Lance', and the second was the *Ko-Hyoteki* midget submarine.

Germany

Germany was the last of the belligerent powers to enter the field of midget submarines. In theory this gave them a position of some advantage in that they could learn a good deal from the experience of their Italian and Japanese allies together with whatever intelligence they had gained of British operational methods and materiel.[4] The German naval attaché in Tokyo, Rear-Admiral Wenneker, was requested to obtain details of the Japanese *Ko-Hyoteki* two-man midget and was provided with a list of forty-six questions to ask concerning its construction. After some hesitation by the Japanese authorities, Wenneker and the Italian naval attaché were allowed to visit Kure on 3 April 1942 where one of the Type A *Ko-Hyoteki*s was paraded for their inspection and Wenneker received the answer to some but not all of his questions. Although Wenneker reported back to Berlin nothing seems to have come of this initiative. Despite the efforts of their allies in this field and the known threat posed by the British, it was not until the end of 1943 that the *Kriegsmarine* began serious investigation of midget submarines. Even then, it was the threat of invasion which provided the stimulus rather than the desire to take the offensive against the Royal Navy.

The *Kriegsmarine* was an intensely conservative force – far more so than the Royal Navy – and commanded by officers with little or no operational or seagoing experience. The weakness at the top in the *Kriegsmarine* is reflected in the often ham-fisted nature in which naval operations were conducted. Their short-sightedness in not investigating midget submarine designs is extremely hard to understand, particularly when one considers that just across the North Sea from the German coastline lay a cornucopia of targets. In the Orkney Islands lay the great harbour of Scapa Flow, further south the naval base at Rosyth, while even closer to Germany lay the port complexes of the Tyne, Humber and Thames. On the English south coast – a short trip from the French coast – were the great naval bases of Portsmouth, Portland and Devonport. Seldom can a belligerent have been presented with such a variety of targets so close to hand.

As invasion forces massed in England the fact slowly dawned on the *Kriegsmarine*'s high command that they had virtually nothing in their armoury with which to oppose a seaborne landing. In order to design and operate such craft, a small unit known as the *Kleinkampfverband* (often abbreviated to *K-Verband*), 'Small Battle Units', was established under the command of Rear-Admiral Helmuth Heye. Heye had previously commanded the cruiser *Admiral Hipper* and had since served in a number of staff appointments and was then Chief of Staff to the Fleet Commander. Heye had been Donitz's original choice for the post but Donitz was persuaded by the Chief of Personnel that Heye could not be spared from his current job. Accordingly Vice-Admiral Weichold was given the job. He was not a success at the job and was speedily relieved by Heye who Donitz described as 'a resourceful man, full of ideas'.[5]

Heye's appointment was unique in that he was simultaneously an operational commander, the representative of his 'service' at the high command and the officer responsible for procurement and production. But as Donitz commented:

> This dual role was unique and was contrary to every principle of organisation. But in this particular case it was a necessary move, designed to ensure the swift raising of a completely novel unit, equipped with completely new kinds of arms.[6]

Heye established the *K-Verband* at a base at Timmersdorfer Strand near Lubeck and this was where the mangled remains of *X6* and *X7* were brought together with the *Welman* captured at Bergen. Heye was unconventional in his approach to training the men of his new command, believing in fostering morale as an essential ingredient to success and thus organised his men very much on the Nelsonian 'Band of Brothers' ethos. There was little formal discipline in the unit, mere lip service was paid to the *Kriegsmarine*'s bureaucracy and rank badges were not worn. There were considerable similarities between the spirit to the *K-Verband* and that of *Decima Mas* but any comparison of the two ends there.

The operations of the various midget submarines during the Second World War remain some of the most supreme examples of cold-blooded courage in history. In a war which became dominated by technology and weapons of mass destruction, the achievements of the midget submariners of all countries stand out and hark back to an earlier and more honourable age, where individual courage and skill-at-arms were the attributes which won wars. Following the failure of the Japanese attack on Sydney, Rear-Admiral Stuart Muirhead-Gould, in charge of the harbour defences, paid the following tribute to the Japanese officers and men who had perished in the attack.

> Theirs was a courage which is not the property, or the tradition or the heritage of any one nation. It is the courage shared by the brave men of our own countries as well of the enemy and, however horrible war and its results may be, it is courage which is recognised and universally admired. These men were patriots of the highest order. How many of us are really prepared to make one thousandth of the sacrifice these men have made?

Those words are a fitting epitaph for all such men.

Human Torpedoes

THE IDEA of attacking the Austrian fleet behind its defences at Pola at the northern end of the Adriatic was first considered by two Italian naval officers, Engineer Lieutenant Commander Raffaele Rossetti and Surgeon Lieutenant Raffaele Paolucci.[1] Rossetti first considered the idea in early June 1915 – not long after Italy had declared war – when Chief Petty Officer Luigi Martignoni, a senior engineering rating onboard the cruiser *Poerio*, asked him if it could be possible to adapt a torpedo to 'human guidance' for an attack against an enemy base. Rossetti was intrigued but it was not until September 1915 that he submitted his idea on paper to his superior, *Colonello del Genio Navale* Giovanni Scialpi. Scialpi was less than impressed and rejected the idea out of hand but indicated that he would not be offended if Rossetti took the proposal to the fleet command.

Therefore on 24 September 1915 Rossetti reported to Vice-Admiral Alberto de Bono, commanding the naval district of La Spezia. De Bono was equally sceptical but advised Rossetti to discuss the matter with the commanding officer of the torpedo trials establishment at La Spezia, *Capitano di Corvetta* Guido Cavalazzi. Cavalazzi merely considered the idea and did nothing, so on 3 November 1915 Rossetti returned to see Admiral de Bono, this time with a detailed memorandum about his project. Rossetti's memorandum stressed the low cost of the project: that two men, wearing diving suits and using a modified Italian B57 torpedo would have an effective range of 30nm. This estimate was a little over-optimistic – as Rossetti realised after the war – and led to the project being turned down by de Bono. When de Bono was relieved by Vice-Admiral Leone Viale in early 1916, Rossetti tried again but found that he was equally unenthusiastic.

For the next two years, Rossetti carried on with work on his project, mostly without the knowledge of his superiors and purloining materials and manpower from other, legitimate, projects to do so. In May 1916 while serving as the Marine Superintendent of the shipyard at Sestri Levante, Rossetti managed to 'obtain' two B57 torpedoes and send them to Genoa. The latter place was not suitable for his purposes so Rossetti managed to have himself transferred to the Materials Trials Commission at La Spezia in May 1917. It was here that the real development work began. Two torpedoes, whose disappearance from Sestri Levante had doubtless been covered by some dubious paperwork, were hidden in the changing room belonging to workers at the submarine base. Some of the workers eagerly joined in the project but before long, the resources available in the changing room proved inadequate and Rossetti approached the commander of the naval air station, let him in on the secret, and succeeded in obtaining the use of a hangar. The web of deceit surrounding the project widened, but higher authority remained blissfully ignorant. The first trials were held on 18 January 1918, and further trials on 24 January and 27 February. The consumption of pressurised air was measured and different types of propellers and diving suits were tested. The last trial, held on 9 March 1918, convinced Rossetti that the device was ready for operations.

The Italian *Mignatta*

The machine, known as *Mignatta* (Leech), was built around a standard B57 14in torpedo, fitted with enlarged 450mm propellers. *Mignatta* would be taken to a point near to Pola by a torpedo-boat. After being lowered into the water it would towed by an MTB to a point as close as they could get to the breakwater without being detected. The two-man 'crew' sat astride the machine, wearing diving suits but no helmets as their heads would be above water. The range of the craft was 10 miles in five hours. The armament was two 170kg warheads which were attached to the target ship by a magnetic clamp. After fixing the warheads the two men would clear the area on the, now lighter, remains of the *Mignatta*.

To get approval for the completed project, Rossetti now had to admit to his clandestine activities over the past two years. His memorandum went as far as Admiral Paolo Thaon di Reval, Commander-in-Chief of the Fleet, who summoned the young engineer to Rome on 1 April 1918. The circumstances of Rossetti's second attempt at getting approval were much more favourable. He now had a machine which worked and could be 'shown off' to the sceptics. Furthermore, by the spring of 1918 Italy had been at war for three years with little to show for it other than lengthening casualty lists. To di Revel and the Italian Naval Staff *Mignatta* seemed the means to strike a blow against the Austrians right in the heart of their most protected anchorage. Thaon di Revel gave a positive response and transferred Rossetti to Venice where he arrived on 5 April. On reporting to the port commander, Captain Constanzo Ciano, Rossetti learned that a group of young officers in Venice were working on similar lines. The Italians were also developing a tracked torpedo-armed assault craft, the *Grillo*, as a means of surmounting the harbour defences of Pola. The first operation using the *Grillo* took place on 13/14 May 1918 and was a disaster, the craft being disabled and the crew taken prisoner.

Rossetti feared that there were too many loose tongues in Venice and that the city was dangerously near the front line. Accordingly he and the *Mignatta* returned to La Spezia. Development and refinement was continuous: a lighter diving suit was designed and tested and on 31 May 1918 Rossetti took the craft on an 8km trip without exhausting the air supply. Rossetti also chose his companion, a young naval surgeon called Raffaele Paolucci. Paolucci's first ride on

Mignatta nearly ended in disaster when the machine turned turtle in the water and Paolucci found himself unable to extricate himself. He was only saved when a nearby salvage vessel was able to pass a strop round *Mignatta* and haul both machine and operator out of the water. Problems with the machine were not the only concern. Relations with Captain Ciano in Venice were deteriorating, as he badly wanted a success to reinforce his position and thus demanded that the attack on Pola be brought forward. Rosetti refused, arguing that it was best to wait until *Mignatta* was perfect.

Events now threatened to overtake Rossetti. On 6 October 1918 the Central Powers approached the United States for a negotiated peace settlement. Di Revel realised that it was, literally, now or never and ordered that the attack was to be launched on the next dark moon period at the beginning of November, regardless of the state of development. Rossetti and the *Mignatta* (of which there were now two, formally named *S1* and *S2*) returned to Venice and on 25 October 1918 carried out a successful trial in which they set off from the Arsenale and attacked a ship moored off the church of Santa Maria Della Salute in the Grand Canal without being observed. Everything was now ready.

On the evening of 31 October 1918 the torpedo boat *PN65* with *S2* on deck and *MAS 95* (a motor torpedo-boat) left Venice. Off Brioni island on the Dalmatian coast, *S2* was lowered into the water and taken in tow by *MAS 95* until they were 66m from the main breakwater outside the harbour at Pola. At 10.13pm *S2* slipped away from *MAS 95* and just after 2.00am on 1 November, they were inside the harbour, having passed the breakwater and clambered over three rows of nets pulling *Mignatta* behind them. Had the defences been in any way alert, the two Italians were bound to have been spotted, but conditions inside the harbour at Pola were anything but normal. The previous day, 30 October, had seen the end of the *Kaiserliche und Konigliche Kriegsmarine* as the Emperor Charles handed over command and control of the fleet to representatives of the South Slav National Council. The actual handover was on 31 October with Admiral Nicholas Horthy leaving the flagship *Viribus Unitis* at 4.45pm after the Austrian colours had been hauled down for the last time. Horthy had been followed by most of the German, Czech and Hungarian nationals (who provided most of the officers and all of the skilled senior ratings in the multi-national Austro-Hungarian Navy), leaving the ships in control of the jubilant Slav remnants of their crews. British signals intelligence personnel at the Italian port of Brindisi, who were monitoring Austrian traffic, heard the port commander at Cattaro ask who was in charge at Pola only to receive the reply, broadcast *en clair* and at full power 'We are!'.[2] *Linienschiffskapitan* Janko Vukovic

The Austrian battleship *Viribus Unitis* sinking at Pola on the morning of 1 November 1918. This 21,000-ton dreadnought battleship, armed with twelve 12in guns, had been sunk by a two-man operated converted torpedo. The sinking of the *Viribus Unitis* was to be inspiration behind much subsequent Italian development in this field. (Author)

de Podkapelski took over as commander-in-chief but failed to restore any sort of order. Despite the fact that no armistice had been arranged with the Allies, the ships were fully illuminated while their crews celebrated, no sentries were posted and none of the ships were maintaining any kind of watertight integrity.

Rossetti and Paolucci were unaware of the political developments taking place around them as they steered *Mignatta* between two rows of brightly illuminated battleships. Unfortunately *Mignatta* began to malfunction. A flooding valve at the stern opened causing the craft to sink and buoyancy could only be restored by using some of the precious air required to propel it. Furthermore they had used more air than they thought in entering the harbour and Rossetti knew that there was not enough left for them to clear the harbour after the attack. Both men would have to abandon *Mignatta* and escape on shore trusting to the local population, many of whom were sympathetic to the Italians.

At 4.30am Rossetti had brought *Mignatta* to the port side of the *Viribus Unitis*. However, on noticing a launch secured to the boom he resolved to let the current take them round the battleship's bows to the starboard side before fixing the warhead. Rossetti separated one warhead from *Mignatta* and secured it to the battleship's side forward of the fourth and fifth 15cm guns. He set a two-hour delay on the fuse, swam back to the *Mignatta* and headed off at full speed leaving a bright fluorescent stern wave. The time was now 5.15am and a bugle call roused the *Viribus Unitis'* crew from their slumbers. It was at this stage that the two Italians were spotted and illuminated with a searchlight. They were wearing rudimentary camouflage intended to disguise themselves as foliage but it was not successful. As a motorboat came toward them, they set the fuse on the other warhead, set the engine to slow speed and gave *Mignatta* a push.

The two Italians were picked out of the water and taken onboard *Viribus Unitis* where their reception was curious but not hostile. Rossetti told de Podkapelski that they had been dropped in the harbour by an aircraft and told him what was about to happen to his ship without being specific. De Podkapelski immediately ordered 'Schiff Verlassen!' (Abandon Ship!) and, unusually for a commanding officer, led his crew and the two Italians over the side. Rossetti and Paolucci were picked up by a boat from the *Tegetthoff*, a sister-ship to the *Viribus Unitis*. When no explosion was observed they were sent back to *Viribus Unitis* where their reception was now very hostile. Both men were stripped of their uniforms and their distinguishing badges of rank. At 6.20am precisely the charge exploded causing the ship to assume an immediate 20° list to starboard. In their anger some of the crew proposed locking Rossetti and Paolucci below decks and letting them drown, but de Podkapelski intervened on their behalf and the two Italians abandoned the *Viribus Unitis* for the second time that morning. Fifteen minutes later the 21,000-ton battleship rolled over and sank. Meanwhile *Mignatta* had been circling round in the current and came to rest under the hull of the liner *Wien* which was serving as a depot ship for German submarine crews. There it exploded, two hours later, causing the *Wien* to sink on an even keel. The exact number who lost their lives on the *Viribus Unitis* is not known. Some estimates are as high as 400 but this is doubtful in view of the reduced ship's company and the fact that most were on the upper deck when the explosion took place. One certain casualty was de Podkapelski who stayed on the bridge of his ship until she sank beneath him.

Rossetti and Paolucci were held captive onboard the old battleship *Habsburg* (used by the Austrians as a prison ship), and later the *Radetzky* before being freed when the Italians occupied Pola on 5 November 1918 after the armistice. Both were subsequently awarded the Cross of the Military Order of Savoy as was Captain Ciano. A subsequent decree awarded the sum of 1,300,000 Lira in gold to be shared between Ciano, Rossetti and Paolucci. Rossetti was outraged that he and Paolucci should have to share their award with Ciano and after a lengthy battle succeeded in having the sum split between him and Paolucci. It would be nice to think that Chief Petty Officer Luigi Martignoni received something but there is no record of any recognition of his role in the affair. The two men subsequently arranged for some of the money to be distributed to the widows of those men killed in the *Viribus Unitis*. It was a gesture typical of the honourable, almost chivalrous spirit which underlay Italian activity in this field of naval operations.

The *Maiale*

Genesis of the design

In October 1935 two engineer officers, Sub-Lieutenants Teseo Tesei and Elios Toschi submitted plans for an improved version of the *Mignatta* to Admiral Cavagnari, Chief of the *Supamarina*, the Italian Naval Staff. Cavagnari approved the idea and work began at La Spezia. Three months later the prototypes were ready. Toschi described the craft as:

> . . . in reality a miniature submarine with entirely novel features, electrical propulsion similar to an aeroplane . . . The crew (pilot and assistant) instead of remained closed and more or less helpless in the interior, keep outside the structure. The two men, true fliers of the sea-depths astride their little underwater aeroplane, are protected by a curved screen of plastic glass . . . At night, under cover of darkness and steering by luminous instruments, they will be able to attack the objective while remaining invisible to the enemy . . . They will be able to cut nets and remove any obstacle with compressed air tools and reach any target . . . with long range breathing sets they can operate at depths down to 30 metres and can carry a powerful explosive charge into an enemy harbour. Invisible and undetectable by the most sensitive acoustic detectors, the operator will be able to penetrate inside the harbour and find the keel of a large ship, attach the charge to it and ensure an explosion will sink the vessel.[3]

There was, however, no requirement for such a craft in Italy's Abyssinian adventure so the weapons were stored and their crews assigned to other duties. But by the summer of 1939 it was clear that a European war was imminent, so the 1st Light Flotilla was formed in June under the command of *Capitan di Fregatta* Paolo Aloisi with instructions to:

> . . . train a nucleus of personnel for employment with given special weapons and of carrying out . . . experiments and tests concerned with perfecting the said weapons.[4]

Aloisi was succeeded in command by *Capitan di Fregatta* Mario Giorgini on the outbreak of war who in turn was succeeded by *Capitan di Fregatta* Vittorio Moccagatta in March 1941. Under Moccagatta's leadership the organisation ceased to be part of the 1st Light Flotilla and became the 10th Light Flotilla, *Decima Mas*, in its own right. This is the name by the which the unit will be referred to in these pages. Moccagatta further split *Decima Mas* into two parts: a surface and a sub-surface weapons group. The former dealt with the operation of the fast explosive motor boats, and the latter with human torpedoes and *Gamma* assault frogmen.

An Italian *Maiale* being swung out of the water in 1942. Note the shrouded propeller, intended to ensure a trouble-free passage through net obstructions. (Dott. Achille Rastelli)

A base was established on a secluded stretch of land on the Boca di Serchio and the officers and men involved in the initial tests were recalled from their units. Cavagnari had taken the decision to order twelve prototypes and at the beginning of 1940 the first successful exercises were held, with the old cruiser *Quarto* as the target, in the Gulf of La Spezia. These were successful and although two of the craft broke down, the third attached a dummy charge to *Quarto* which would certainly have resulted in her destruction. The concept had become a reality. However, the loss of two years' research and development time meant that when Italy declared war on 10 June 1940, the weapon was still in an experimental stage and few were available for operations.

Construction and machinery

What was the craft which *Decima Mas* was to operate so successfully? It was officially known as *Siluro a Lenta Corsa* (SLC),[5] but the name by which they will

An alternative view of a *Maiale* looking down the starboard side. Note the extreme simplicity of construction with all services being run externally down the 'hull'. (Dott. Achille Rastelli)

Looking forward along the *Maiale*'s side, this photograph shows the simple control instruments positioned under the 'hood'. (Dott. Achille Rastelli)

be forever be known is *Maiale* ('Pig'). During early trials Tesei had to abandon a sinking SLC and came to the surface with the words, 'That swine got away!'. The name stuck. The craft was 7.3m long overall which included the 300kg warhead at the front which was 1.8m long. The diameter of the craft was 0.53m.

The two operators sat astride the craft, the driver in front with the No.2 behind. Beneath the driver's seat was the forward trimming tank. Between and beneath the two seats was the battery consisting of thirty 60v cells. At a speed of 4.5kts the *Maiale* had a range of 4 miles and at 2.3kts 15 miles. Inside the after portion of

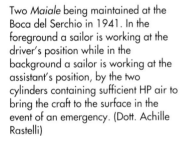

Two *Maiale* being maintained at the Boca del Serchio in 1941. In the foreground a sailor is working at the driver's position while in the background a sailor is working at the assistant's position, by the two cylinders containing sufficient HP air to bring the craft to the surface in the event of an emergency. (Dott. Achille Rastelli)

the craft was the 1.1hp (later increased to 1.6hp) electric motor and the stern trimming tank. At the stern was the propeller, with hydroplanes and a vertical rudder, both surrounded by a protective shroud.[6]

The two operators sat behind shields to lessen the water resistance. The driver controlled the craft by means of a joystick which worked both rudder and hydroplanes. Speed was regulated by a fly-wheel connected to a rheostat. Between the two operators was the quick-diving tank which was flooded by lever action from the No.2's position and blown by compressed air from a compressed air cylinder. Behind the No.2's seat was a locker containing net cutters, a set of working tools, plenty of rope and clamps used to attach the warhead to the hull of the target. The operators wore a one-piece 'Belloni' suit and breathed oxygen through a closed-cycle breathing apparatus (*Austorespiratore ad Ossigeno*) which left no tell-tale trail of bubbles on the surface. The apparatus consisted of two high-pressure oxygen cylinders which gave about 6 hours' breathing time. The oxygen was fed, via a reducing valve and a flexible tube, into the operator's mouthpiece. The operator exhaled through the same tube and the 'exhaust' air was cleaned in a cylinder containing soda lime crystals.

The 300kg warhead (some later *Maiale* could carry two 150kg charges) at the front of the craft was held in position by a metal clutch. The procedure for attach-

ing the warhead to the target was for the driver to position the *Maiale* directly under one of the target's bilge keels. The No.2 would then dismount and secure a clamp to the keel to which was attached a length of rope. The driver would then move the *Maiale* forward under the hull while the diver swam

The Italian submarine *Gondar* showing the two *Maiale* containers on the forward casing. (Dott. Achille Rastelli)

Storage containers for *Maiale* on the after casing of the Italian submarine *Scire*. The *Maiale* rested on the wooden boards at the bottom of the container. (Dott. Achille Rastelli)

The submarine *Ambra* showing her arrangement of two *Maiale* containers aft and one forward. (Dott. Achille Rastelli)

round and attached another clamp to the bilge keel on the other side of the hull. He would then return and attach both cables firmly to the warhead and set the fuse – a setting of 2½ hours' delay was possible. When all was secure, he would give the appropriate signal and the driver would release the warhead, so that it hung under the target's hull, suspended from the bilge keels. The operators would then get clear.

Modus operandi

Initially the Italians thought of delivering the *Maiale* to the operational area by air using a Cant Z.511 flying-boat. This idea was swiftly abandoned, although it is interesting to note that in turn the British and Germans both considered the possibility of delivering underwater assault craft by air. Instead Aloisi turned

An alternative arrangement, though never operationally deployed, was to have the containers mounted on the saddle tanks as shown in this photograph of the launch of *Murena* on 11 April 1943. (Dott. Achille Rastelli)

Mk I Chariot General Arrangement

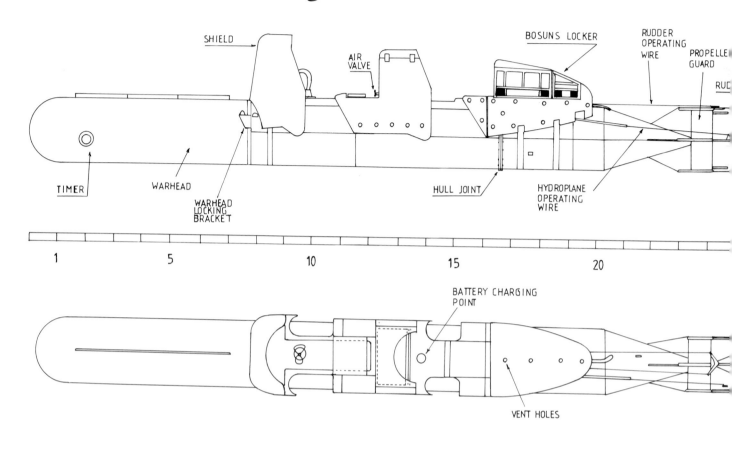

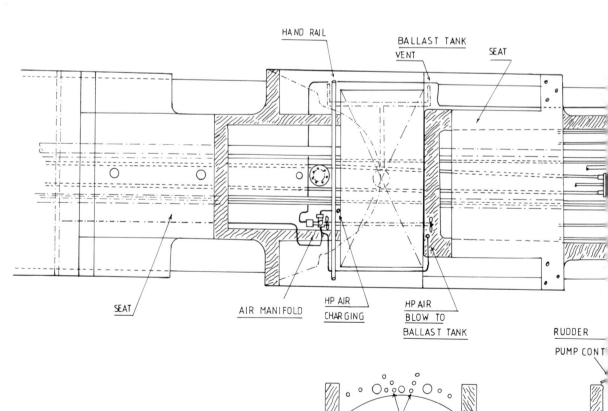

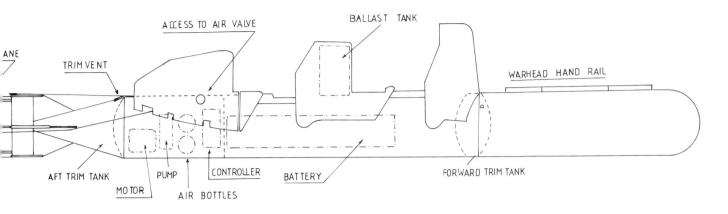

ANE

ACCESS TO AIR VALVE

TRIM VENT

BALLAST TANK

WARHEAD HAND RAIL

AFT TRIM TANK

MOTOR

PUMP

AIR BOTTLES

CONTROLLER

BATTERY

FORWARD TRIM TANK

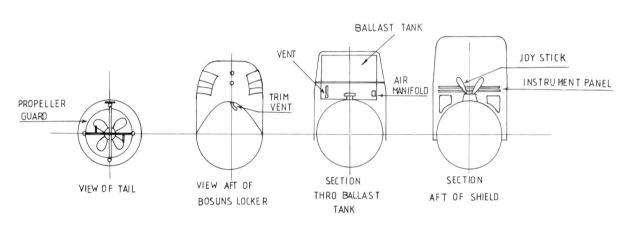

PROPELLER GUARD

VIEW OF TAIL

VIEW AFT OF BOSUNS LOCKER

TRIM VENT

VENT

BALLAST TANK

AIR MANIFOLD

SECTION THRO BALLAST TANK

JOY STICK

INSTRUMENT PANEL

SECTION AFT OF SHIELD

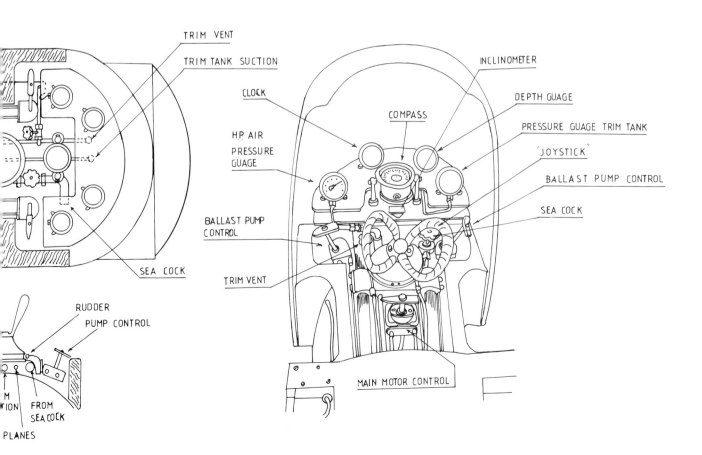

TRIM VENT

TRIM TANK SUCTION

CLOCK

H.P AIR PRESSURE GUAGE

BALLAST PUMP CONTROL

TRIM VENT

SEA COCK

RUDDER

PUMP CONTROL

M
TION

FROM SEA COCK

PLANES

INCLINOMETER

COMPASS

DEPTH GUAGE

PRESSURE GUAGE TRIM TANK

JOYSTICK

BALLAST PUMP CONTROL

SEA COCK

MAIN MOTOR CONTROL

The exit/re-entry port cut in the bow of the tanker *Olterra* to allow *Maiale* and *Gamma* frogmen to leave the tanker for attacks on shipping at Gibraltar. The photograph was taken after *Olterra* came into British hands in September 1943 and shows the tanker heavily ballasted by the stern so as to bring the port above water. (Dott. Achille Rastelli)

to the submarine as the most likely means of delivery. The old boat *Ametista* was fitted with pressure-tight containers on her casing in which the *Maiale* would be kept on passage. When the submarine was near the target area, the *Maiale* would be removed from the containers and released to proceed on their own. Following the success of trials with *Ametista*, three such containers were fitted to the submarines *Iride*, *Gondar*, *Scire* and *Ambra*. Initially the submarine would surface to launch the SLCs, but the Italians quickly developed quite sophisticated exit/re-entry techniques so that the operators would leave the parent boat through the fore hatch while it was submerged. This, of course, reduced the risk of the boat being caught on the surface with the containers open and the *Maiale* and their crews on the casing. An important feature of the *Maiale* containers was that they were built to the same constructional standards as the submarine's hull so that the commanding officer would not have his freedom of action constrained

A cheerful Chief Petty Officer crouches in *Olterra*'s exit/re-entry port. (Royal Navy Submarine Museum 8273)

by carrying them. An alternative option was the use of a specially converted motor boat, *Motosiluranti*. Two such MTBs were converted and could carry a *Maiale* on a specially-configured stern ramp, from which it would be slid into the water stern first.

A feature of *Maiale* operations was the development of covert bases near to the British base at Gibraltar. The Italians reasoned that to maximise the use of the *Maiale* it was uneconomic and risky to deploy them from a large transport submarine for every operation. Targets reported by Italian coastwatchers in Spain might have moved on by the time the submarine reached the area, and furthermore the operators got 'stale' in the passage to the target area. What was wanted was a base on the British doorstep from which they could launch repeated attacks with impunity.

They were fortunate in that the Spanish authorities turned a blind eye to their activities. For Operation BG.3 in May 1941 the *Maiale* operators went overland to the Italian tanker *Fulgor* from which they transferred to the submarine. The same *modus operandi* was used in Operation BG.4 in September 1941. But the *Decima Mas* planners, and a young *Maiale* operator TV Licio Visintini, wanted to take this idea one stage further and develop a fully-operational *Maiale* base overlooking Gibraltar harbour. For this purpose neither the *Fulgor* nor the Villa Carmela–a house in Algeciras also used by Italian *Gamma* swimmers to attack shipping at Gibraltar–were suitable. The *Fulgor* lay too far away at Cadiz and, in any case, any attempt to move her nearer to Gibraltar would arouse the suspicion of the British. The Villa Carmela was

suitable as a temporary holding point for *Gamma* men but could not be used regularly for operations and it would be out of the question to take *Maiale* directly to the beach for launching from there. Such a course of action would stretch the patience of the Spanish authorities too far.

Instead Visintini focused on the Italian tanker *Olterra* lying at Algeciras. She had been scuttled by her Italian crew on the outbreak of war but had been refloated by the Spanish and secured inside the breakwater. A guard consisting of a corporal and four privates of the *Guardia Civilia* was mounted to prevent all unauthorised personnel boarding the ship. In March 1941 members of the *Olterra*'s original crew including Paolo Denegri, the Chief Engineer, returned the ship to act as a care and maintenance party. The Italians were provided with special passes allowing them to board the ship.[7] Visintini arrived onboard *Olterra* on 27 June 1942 with civilian papers identifying him as Lino Valeri, the prospective First Officer of the *Olterra*. He brought three technicians with him and also a medical technician. These four men were to become the core of the *Olterra*'s *Decima Mas* detachment and would remain on the ship until operations ceased in September 1943. Visintini lost no time in getting to work. Four members of the *Olterra*'s mercantile crew were transferred to another ship on the grounds that they were indiscreet. At the same time Visintini banned the Spanish guards from visiting the forward part of the ship on the grounds that he suspected them of stealing food. Denegri and the three 'technicians' fulfilled a number of roles. Preparing the

The forepeak of the tanker *Olterra* showing the access hole cut through to the secret exit/re-entry compartment in the bow. *Maiale* were swung through into this compartment by block and tackle slung from the beams on the deckhead. The photograph was taken after the ship had been handed over to the British and after the Italians had unsuccessfully tried to wreck the interior. (Author)

Maiale was their most important function together with acting as 'dressers' for the operators, but they also under took a number of other tasks including daytime reconnaissance of shipping in Gibraltar (they were often spotted by British agents doing this) by telescope from the ship's bridge and acting as enforcers to keep away any curious Spaniards.

With the unreliable elements of the crew dismissed and the Spanish guard confined to the stern, Visintini briefed those remaining on *Olterra's* new role as a base for *Maiale* operations against Gibraltar. In order to facilitate operations of the *Maiale* a forward bulkhead was cut and hinged to give access to the forepeak. Torpedo racks were manufactured ashore in Algeciras and assembled in the forepeak. Finally the tanker was trimmed down by the stern to allow the cutting of a hinged trapdoor measuring 5ft x 8ft in the hull. The cutting took about two hours after which the trim was returned to normal so that the opening was hidden below the waterline. The cutting party was hidden by pontoons and stages moored alongside for painting and minor repairs to the ship's hull. Cables for charging batteries were brought from the dynamos at the stern concealed inside water pipes. The *Maiale* were broken down into their component parts and packed into wooden crates, together with mines, *Belloni* suits, clamps, oxygen cylinders and all the other equipment needed for *Maiale* operations, and shipped to Algeciras by road directly from Italy. Some of the crates were labelled as engineering spares and at least one box was filled with boiler tubes and left with one end opened for the benefit of the curious. Other material was collected by Denegri from the Italian Embassy in Madrid where it had been sent by diplomatic courier. On another occasion a member of *Olterra's* crew was granted compassionate leave to return to Italy. On his return he brought a crate of limpet mines with him. The arrival of such a large amount of equipment officially destined for a derelict tanker did not apparently arouse the slightest suspicion or concern among the Spanish authorities. The use of the *Olterra* as a covert base for *Maiale* operations was and remains one of the most audacious stories of the Second World War.

Maiale operations

The *Regia Marina* employed *Maiale* against British targets at Alexandria and Gibraltar. Space precludes a description of such operations and excellent accounts exist in both English and Italian. The table below gives a list of their successes but does scant justice to the effect these operations had on the British. The *Maiale* and their operators were rightly respected. In 1943 a young Italian naval officer, Gino Birindelli, who been captured during the *Maiale* attack on Gibraltar in October 1940, was due to be repatriated to Italy on health grounds. Just as he was about to set foot on the repatriation ship, he was seized by Military Police and put on the next POW transport to Canada. The Admiralty considered that even in his weakened condition he could not be allowed to return to Italy to give others the benefit of his experience.

Table 1: *Maiale* operations

Date	Codename	Target	Result
21 Aug 1940	GA.1	Alexandria	Cancelled
29 Sep 1940	GA.2	Alexandria	Transport S/M *Gondar* sunk
29 Sep 1940	BG.1	Gibraltar	Cancelled
30 Oct 1940	BG.2	Gibraltar	No result: two *Maiale* escaped to Spain, the third sank and crew captured.
25 May 1941	BG.3	Gibraltar	No result. All three *Maiale* crews escaped to Spain.
26 Jul 1941		Malta	Two *Maiale* lost
19 Sep 1941	BG.4	Gibraltar	2444GRT *Fiona Shell*, 10,900GRT *Durham* and 8145GRT *Denbydale* sunk. All three *Maiale* crews escaped to Spain.
19 Dec 1941	GA.3	Alexandria	Battleships *Queen Elizabeth* and *Valiant* damaged, together with tanker *Sagona*. All six *Maiale* operators taken prisoner.
29 Apr 1942	GA.3	Alexandria	Abandoned.
7 Dec 1942	BG.5	Gibraltar	No result. Of the six *Maiale* operators, one escaped to Spain, three killed/ missing and two taken prisoner.
7/8 May 1943	BG.6	Gibraltar	7191GRT *Son*, 7540GRT *Mahsud* and 4875GRT *Camerata* damaged. All three *Maiale* crews escaped.
3/4 Aug 1943	BG.7	Gibraltar	9444GRT *Thorshivdi*, 5975GRT *Stanridge* and 7176GRT *Harrison Grey Otis* damaged. Five of the six operators escaped to Spain.

Keeping up appearances: Admiral Sir Andrew Cunningham takes the salute at the morning ceremony of 'Colours'. This photograph was taken for the benefit of the press to show all was well and hid the fact that his flagship, HMS *Queen Elizabeth*, was resting on the bottom following the *Maiale* attack of the night of 19 December 1941. (Author)

but ultimately it could never be more than a highly effective irritant. Nevertheless the Italian flair for this sort of underwater warfare had been amply demonstrated.

The British Chariot

It was the exploits of the Italians in the Mediterranean which encouraged the British toward the development of underwater assault craft. Nothing succeeds like success and the British were thoroughly irritated by the activities of the Italians in the Mediterranean which, of course, had culminated in the crippling of the battleships *Valiant* and *Queen Elizabeth* at Alexandria on the night of 20/21 December 1941. Winston Churchill was never one to have his thinking restrained by conventional dogma and on 18 January the familiar '*Action this Day*' docket landed on the desk of General Sir Hastings Ismay, Secretary to the Chiefs of Staff Committee:

> Please report what is being done to emulate the exploits of the Italians in Alexandria harbour and similar methods of this kind. At the beginning of the war Colonel Jefferis had a number of bright ideas on this subject which received very little encouragement. Is there any reason why we should be incapable of the same kind of scientific aggressive action the Italians have shown? One would have thought that we would have been in the lead.[8]

In due course the requirement landed on the desk of Vice-Admiral Max Horton, Flag Officer Submarines. Horton sent for Commander W R 'Tiny' Fell, a submariner and old acquaintance, and ordered him to:

> Go away and build me a Human Torpedo. I'm busy but get on with the job right away and report to me as soon as you have got something.[9]

Horton was a commander who never wasted a moment on complicated staff requirements. The job needed to be done and having delegated, Horton expected results.

Fell was a submariner who had thought that his submarine days were over when he handed over command of *H-31* in August 1939. Shortly after the declaration of war Fell was appointed to command the submarine *H-43* which together with the trawler *Tamura* spent the winter of 1939-40 in a fruitless and

This is an impressive total under any circumstances but reflecting on these operations, Admiral Gino Birindelli, who had been captured in Operation BG.2, considered that the Italians failed to make the most of this weapon. *Decima Mas Maiale* attacks were planned to inflict the maximum damage possible but little or no consideration was to given to the wider Axis plan of campaign. Birindelli offers the opinion that the successful GA.3 operation, if combined with a successful land offensive, could have had effects out of all proportion to the scale of the operation. Sadly Italy's lack of economic muscle and shortage of strategic materials did not permit this sort of grandiose planning. *Decima Mas* had the capacity to be a strategic weapon

British 'Chariot' two-man human torpedo.

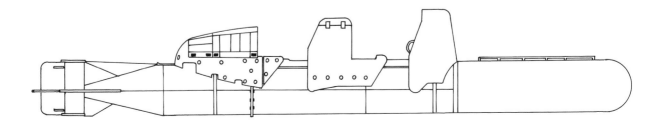

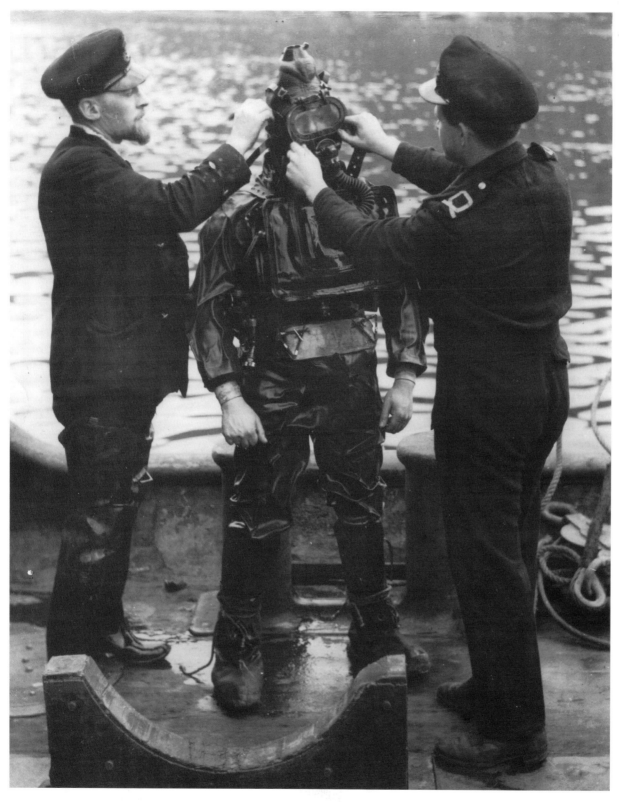

A British 'Charioteer' being helped into his 'Clammy Death' suit before a training operation. The breathing suit on his chest was adapted from the Davis Submarine Escape Apparatus used by submariners. Note the bare hands – gloves were provided with the suit but many operators chose not to wear them since they were so cumbersome. To keep out the cold many 'Charioteers' chose to coat their hands in thick engine grease. (Author)

uncomfortable search for U-boats suspected to be lurking in Irish territorial waters.[10] Thereafter he had been employed in combined operations and seen service at the raids on Vaagsoy and Floro. Though he found these exciting, he was casting about for a return to his beloved submarine service when Horton sent for him. He proceeded to HMS *Dolphin* at Gosport, the home of the Submarine Service. where he joined Commander Geoffrey Sladen, an experienced subma-

rine commander who had just relinquished command of HMS *Trident* after a very successful commission in Arctic waters. Sladen concentrated on the development of a flexible underwater suit with air supplied by an oxygen bag similar to the Davis Submarine Escape Apparatus in general use throughout the Navy. The breathing apparatus was a closed-cycle one, that is that the air was recycled within the equipment and not vented where it would leave a trail of bubbles, thus giving the game away. The breathing bag contained a cylinder which supplied the wearer with pure oxygen. On exhaling the air was passed through protosorb crystals which removed most of the CO_2. The dangers of breathing pure oxygen were not fully appreciated by the British, although the Italian *Decima MAS* men were well aware of such problems. British interrogation of Italian operators put this caution down to poor training.[11] This was not the case: the Italians were more aware of these dangers as the result of some singularly brutal peacetime experiments. The suit became known as the 'Clammy Death' suit and consisted of a one-piece rubber body overall and hood. Early models had individual eye goggles but later versions were fitted with a single visor over which a pair of night vision glasses could be fitted. One problem that had to be solved at the beginning was what underclothing to wear which would keep the wearer warm without encumbering him too much. Various combinations were tried and the favoured was silk underwear next to the skin, woollen underwear worn over that and kapok-padded jerkins and trousers worn under the suit. No satisfactory means could be found of keeping the Charioteers' hands warm. No gloves seemed up to the task and eventually Sladen left each man to make his own choice. Most opted for bare hands with a liberal measure of heavy-duty grease. Whatever the apparent glamour of serving in aspecial unit, Charioteering was never a pleasant experience:

With nose tightly clipped for hours, swollen and raw from the previous day's dive, with gums cut and puffed from constant gripping of the mouthpiece, and with hands cold to the point of numbness, cut and torn from each day's diving . . . And when one surfaced, and hands thawed out while one undressed, there was the feeling that all hell had broken loose with the remaining circulation.[12]

Meanwhile Fell was building the first prototype out of a 20ft log of wood ably assisted by Engineer Commander Stan Kerry, the base engineer officer. Fortunately Fell and Kerry had plans and photographs of an Italian *Maiale* captured at Gibraltar. Building a Chariot[13] did not present any serious engineering problems and after a number of experiments on a wooden prototype dignified by the name of *Cassidy*, the first powered craft was ready in June 1942. The machine was 7.65m long and resembled a standard 21in torpedo except that positions for the two crew had been built on top and that the nose had fittings to hold the 600lb detachable warhead. The 60v lead acid battery containing 30 chloride cells drove the 2hp motor along at 4kts for four hours and for six hours at just under 3kts. In theory this provided for an operational range of 18 miles. The battery also supplied the power for the ballast and trim pump motors.

The pilot, 'Number One', sat forward behind a breast-high screen which covered his rudimentary

'Number One' sits at his position on a Chariot, which is not fitted with a warhead. He is shown holding the 'helm' which controlled the rudder and the hydroplanes. (Royal Navy Submarine Museum 0360)

Another view of 'Number One' at his position. Behind 'Number One' was the ballast tank while behind 'Number Two' was a locker containing net cutters and other items of equipment. (Royal Navy Submarine Museum 0406A)

By way of comparison with the previous Italian arrangements, this photograph shows the British HMS/M *Trooper* fitted with containers for carrying Chariots. The broad after casing of the later 'T' class submarines made a very suitable platform for Chariot-carrying. (Author)

instruments: a depth gauge, compass and clock. Between his knees was the helm which operated the rudder and hydroplanes (one set mounted aft). To the left and right of the helm were switches controlling the ballast and trim pump while behind it was the main motor switch. Number One's back rested against the main ballast tank which also served as protection for the diver, Number Two, straddling the after end of the machine. In turn Number Two rested against a locker containing net cutters, ropes and two spare sets of breathing apparatus.

As the Italians had done (and the Germans would in time), the British considered delivering the Chariot to the operational area by aircraft. Operation 'Large Lumps' involved slinging a Chariot under each wing of a Sunderland flying-boat. For obvious practical reasons the plan was quickly consigned to oblivion. Carrying the Chariot slung in davits in an MTB was another alternative. But as with the Italians, it was the submarine which offered the ideal combination of flexibility, endurance and security. Three 'T' class submarines, *Trooper*, *Thunderbolt* and *P.311* were taken in hand for conversion in which pressure-tight containers for the Chariots were welded onto their casings. *Thunderbolt* and *P.311* carried two Chariots each – one forward and one aft of the conning tower – while *Trooper* carried one forward and two aft. The launching drill would be for the submarine to surface, after making all the usual precautions that it was safe to do so. The Charioteers would already be dressed in their 'Clammy Death' suits and accompanied by their 'dressers' would clamber up and out of the conning tower and down onto the casing – no easy task when thus encumbered. The submarine would then trim down to bring the containers awash. The dressers would open the containers and drag the Chariots out. As they came clear the Charioteers would climb on and proceed. It sounds very simple but it was an extremely dangerous time for the submarine. There was constant risk that she might be surprised on the surface with the containers open and all manner of people stranded on the casing. Everything depended on the vigilance of the lookouts for although an listening watch would be kept on the ASDIC, that apparatus would be next to useless given the background of sea noise. Although submarines like *Thunderbolt* were fitted with the fairly basic Type 291W air-warning radar, its performance was indifferent at the best of times. Moreover, there were fears that the Italians possessed radar-warning receivers. A refinement of this technique, developed in June 1943, was for the charioteers to use the two-man escape chambers fitted in the 'T' class to leave and re-enter the submarine while she remained dived, thus removing the need for the boat to surface. Although an ingenious idea, it proved impractical when tried in HMS *Truant*. There was barely enough space in the chamber for two men

wearing normal clothing let alone a Charioteer and his dresser wearing diving suits. Nevertheless, the experiment paved the way for the development of exit/re-entry compartments which are so common in modern submarines.[14]

Attacking the *Tirpitz* deep in her Norwegian lair posed special problems. The battleship lay holed up deep in a fjord far from the sea. No submarine could penetrate the fjord and it was beyond the endurance of a Chariot to go the distance alone. Accordingly a Norwegian trawler, the *Arthur*, was modified so that two Chariots could be slung underneath her hull and so securely that they could remain there throughout a crossing of the North Sea. The operators would evade the German patrols by hiding in a specially-constructed compartment. The idea was brilliant but impractical. When used operationally the tethers holding the Chariots to *Arthur*'s hull broke and the Chariots sank to the bottom.

Trials and training

Initial trials at Portsmouth were successful but it was not easy to work up the craft in that crowded harbour with all sorts of interested (friendly or otherwise) spectators. Consequently the Chariots and operators moved north to Scotland, first to Erisart (found unsuitable) and then to Loch Cairnbawn. The ancient depot ship HMS *Titania* was allocated to support the Chariots but her commanding officer, Commander Robert Conway RN, was less than impressed with his new charges, following news that the Charioteers had held a party *underneath* the train while waiting to depart from Euston and had only been dissuaded by the arrival of Admiral Horton who was, coincidentally (and unfortunately) taking the First Lord of the Admiralty,[15] the Hon. A V Alexander (a singularly humourless character at the best of times) to visit the Submarine Flotillas in Scotland.

Once in Scotland training began with a vengeance. The Boom Defence Department laid on various types of net for the Charioteers to work with and gradually their skills were perfected. However, the curriculum established by Sladen and Fell was by no means confined to the aquatic aspect of the task in hand. There was always the prospect of his men being forced to escape overland after an operation. As a result he suggested to the local Home Guard commander that they run an escape and evasion exercise. The result was pure unadulterated mayhem, the climax of which was the passing of a calcium flare, which had just been dipped in water, through the letterbox of the local police station.

The climax of all this training was a series of exercises against a 'live' target. The battleship HMS *Howe* was obligingly loaned by the Home Fleet and after her arrival in Loch Cairnbawn she was immediately surrounded by a few layers of nets supplemented by hydrophones rigged out on booms and suspended from the ship's side. Additionally her boats would patrol between the ship and net and would be carrying Aldis lamps to use as searchlights. Seven Chariots left *Titania* at 15-minute intervals with the simple instruction from Fell and Sladen, 'Get your charge under the *Howe* and get away undetected'. It was a tall order: the defences were tougher than anything the Charioteers had faced so far, the loch was littered with pockets of fresh water and, unknown to Sladen and Fell, *Howe*'s draught was deeper than the safe depth for breathing oxygen under pressure.

The exercise was a complete success: three of the Chariots planted their charges and returned, a fourth being spotted by the launch on the way out. The other three Chariots were all forced to withdraw for various technical reasons but none were spotted. Had the attack been a real one there was no doubt that *Howe* would have been sunk. However, the exercise revealed some hazards of 'Charioteering': Lieutenant S F Stretton-Smith RNVR and Leading Seaman Rickman hit an unexpected pocket of fresh water and crashed some 70ft to the bottom and had to be rested for several days to allow their ears to recover from the ordeal. The operation was repeated on the following night and was just as sucessful: four machines were used and all four planted their charges although two were spotted on the way out. The second exercise was enlivened by Lieutenant D C 'Taffy' Evans RNVR and Petty Officer W S Smith placing their charge underneath the accommodation ladder leading up to the quarterdeck under the very eyes of the officer of the watch.

There was time for one more exercise before *Howe* had to sail for more conventional duties. Before this the Chariots ran up and down the line of hydrophones to provide information about the noise they generated. During these trials, carried out in daylight, *Howe*'s upper deck was cleared of all but those whose duties were concerned with the working of the ship or the trials themselves. On the third attack, tragedy struck. It was perhaps too much for all to have gone so well without serious accident. While underneath the 35,000-ton battleship fixing his mine, Sub-Lieutenant Jack Grogan SANVR passed out. His Number Two, Able Seaman 'Geordie' Worthy, acted quickly by taking control and moving forward and out from underneath *Howe*'s hull and thence to the surface. For all his efforts it was too late: Grogan was dead, probably as a result of oxygen poisoning. One death and the various *materiel* failures were to be expected given the hazardous and experimental nature of Charioteering. In a real operation there would certainly be greater losses.

Operations

British Chariot operations did not fulfil the high expectations had of them. The machine was not a success in cold northern waters – the one operation

Two Charioteers prepare to board their craft – note their bare hands. (Royal Navy Submarine Museum 3673)

against the *Tirpitz* was abandoned when the Chariots broke away from their parent craft. In the Mediterranean they achieved some success at Palermo, where a light cruiser and merchant ship were damaged, and at Tripoli but at some cost – the submarine *Traveller* was lost in a reconnaissance of Taranto harbour before Operation 'Principal' while *P.311* was lost in the operation itself. At a time when

Number Two is opening a small locker positioned above the ballast tank that also served as a backrest for Number One. (Royal Navy Submarine Museum 7539)

A Chariot under way in a Scottish loch in 1942. Note how little of the craft is visible even when she is running on the surface. (Royal Navy Submarine Museum 1793)

every submarine was, in the words of Admiral Sir Andrew Cunningham (no great admirer of the submarine service), 'Worth her weight in gold', it was a high price to pay. This opinion was shared by Commander Simpson who as commanding officer of the 10th Submarine Flotilla, the 'Fighting Tenth', was responsible for the prosecution of the submarine war in the central Mediterranean:

If it [Operation 'Principal'] only resulted in the sinking of a light cruiser not yet in commission and an 8,500 ton transport, then the prolonged use of three T-Class submarines exclusively for Chariot work and the loss of one of them, seems a disproportionate price to have paid.[16]

There were two other Chariot operations in the Mediterranean. On 18 January 1943 two Chariots launched by HMS *Thunderbolt* were sent to sink merchant ships to prevent their use as blockships by the Germans at Tripoli on the North African coast.

Table 2: *Chariot* operations

Date	Codename	Target	Result
1 Nov 1942	'Title'	*Tirpitz*	Aborted when Chariots broke away from *Arthur*.
2/3 Jan 1943	'Principal'	Palermo	Cruiser *Ulpio Traiano* and liner *Viminale* damaged
18 Jan 1943		Tripoli	Blocking of harbour prevented.
May/June 1943		Sicily	Beach reconnaissance
Oct 1943		Norway	Abandoned – when MTB detected
27 Oct 1944		Penang	Liners *Volpi* and *Sumatra* damaged

The other Chariot operation in the Mediterranean was a new departure for these craft in that they undertook reconnaissance of the invasion beaches before the invasion of Sicily in May and June 1943. For these operations one Chariot was carried on the casing of the 'U' class submarines *Unrivalled*, *Unseen* and *Unison*. The operations yielded extremely useful hydrographic data but as Captain G C Phillips RN, Captain (S)10 noted:

> It is hoped that that these reconnaissances are of real value to the planners. It has become clear from recent results that submarines engaged on reconnaissance work fall off in efficiency for offensive patrols.[17]

Beach reconnaissance prior to the invasion of Sicily marked the end of Chariot operations in the Mediterranean (except for the unique Anglo-Italian operation in June 1944). Amazingly new Chariots and more personnel were sent out to the Mediterranean even when it was clear that there was no employment for them. Much time was spent in grandiose schemes for blocking the Corinth Canal and for attacking the Italian battlefleet in Taranto but with the Italian capitulation in September 1943, all these schemes came to an end. There was only one more Chariot operation in the Second World War. This took place in the Far East against two Italian liners lying at Phuket north of Penang on 27 October 1944. Potentially the Far East offered considerable opportunity for Chariot operations in view of Japan's large naval and mercantile fleet. After due consideration however, the Admiralty decided that the Chariots should be withdrawn from the theatre since:

The explosion of a 600lb Chariot warhead. (Royal Navy Submarine Museum 10777)

> ... although targets exist, they do not afford that reasonable prospect of escape for Charioteers which is essential when dealing with an inhuman enemy.[18]

The Phuket operation marked the end of the Royal Navy's involvement with Chariots. The experience

A post-war view of the Chariot Mk.II in which operators sat back to back in an enclosed cockpit. It was craft of this type which carried out the attack on Phuket Harbour on 27 October 1944. (Author)

Looking down on the Chariot Mk.II from the depot ship, this photograph gives a good view of the cockpit. (Royal Navy Submarine Museum 8936)

was not wholly wasted since the knowledge gained was applied with equal success to the rapidly expanding field of assault frogmen and clearance diving. It is doubtful whether the Chariots repaid their inventors' hopes or the investment in terms of materiel. They had been built to take on the *Tirpitz* and following the failure of the sole operation against that target, they were flung willy-nilly at whatever target presented itself. Their exploits in the Mediterranean, gallant though they undoubtedly were, were hardly war-winning stuff and the loss of two conventional submarines in support of Chariot operations was certainly not an acceptable exchange. Chariots were an imaginative but ill-conceived response to a particular threat.

Post-1945 developments

One aspect of midget submarine operations which has survived almost unaltered since the Second World War is a successor to the wartime *Maiale* and *Chariots*, now known as Swimmer Delivery Vehicles (SDV). These are now far more sophisticated than the weapons in which Greenland and Visintini went to war but the basic principles are the same. They can be carried by submarines—a number of former SSBNs 'disarmed' by the SALT and START agreements are enjoying a new lease of life as assault swimmer carriers. USS *Sam Houston* (SSBN 609) and *John Marshall* (SSBN 611) of the *Ethan Allen* class were converted to carry sixty-seven SEAL swimmers in double dry-deck shelters fixed to the casing when it proved impossible to replace their Polaris missiles with the larger Poseidon system. Conversion started in 1984 but both boats were decommissioned in September and November 1991 respectively. They were replaced by the *Kamehameha* (SSBN 642) and the *James Polk* (SSBN 645) of the *Lafayette* class. On the Soviet side a number of Project 66 and 66A boats (better known the west as the 'Yankee' SSBN) have been refitted for other duties by having their central section (containing the sixteen SS-N-4 missiles) removed and the two halves of the boat welded together. Nearly all modern

submarines have escape chambers which can easily double as exit/re-entry chambers for divers while some 'conventional' submarines, such as the British *Otus* and *Opossum* were fitted with five-man exit/re-entry chambers built into their fins. Whatever the refinements made to the *materiel* in modern submarines, the principles are the same as those under which *Decima Mas* operated so successfully. There is nothing much in the midget submarine world that has not been done before.

Yugoslavia has been the principle exporter of midget submarines in the post-war period. The Tito government developed an export-orientated arms industry as a means of earning foreign exchange, their main clients being countries whose financial or political credentials made them *persona non grata* with the major western or eastern bloc suppliers. The Yugoslavs developed three different models: the R1 one-man SDV, the R2 two-man SDV and the *Una* class midget submarine. The R1 is a single seat underwater vehicle for one frogman and can be used for underwater reconnaissance and the surveillance of minefields. It is of monohull construction with ballast tanks at the bow and stern. It can be transported in a standard torpedo tube and used both in fresh water and in sea water with a specific gravity of 1.000-1.030 t/m^3 without reserve uplift. The craft can dive to a depth of 60m and is powered by a 1kw electric motor supplied by a 24v DC silver-zinc battery. Endurance is measured at 6nm at 3kts and 8nm at 2.5kts. The single operator lies along the top of the craft, rather than sitting astride it as in the wartime *Maiale*, and is provided with a gyro-magnetic compass, sonar, echo sounder, electric clock and other instruments.

The R2 *Mala* is a spindle-shaped craft seating two divers side by side and has the same roles as the R1, but carries two 50kg limpet mines. The hull is made of aluminium alloy resistant to seawater corrosion. Submerged control is by fore and aft hydroplanes, the tail being a conventional cruciform with a rudder fitted aft of the three-bladed screw. The front upper part of the craft is made of plexiglass. The hull can be fully flooded except for the cylinders containing the 24v storage battery, the 4.5kw electric motor, navigational instruments and ballast tanks. The navigational equipment is contained in a watertight housing and consists of a gyro-magnetic compass, depth gauge, echo-sounder, sonar and two searchlights. The craft can be carried on a submarine's casing or as deck cargo in any ship with a 25-ton crane. *Mala*s have been sold to Sweden (where they function in the role of loyal opposition, training Swedish ASW forces), the USSR and Libya. The Libyans have six of these craft. Although none of the ships in the Libyan Navy is capable of carrying a *Mala* there is no reason why any of the ships in the Libyan merchant marine[19] should not be converted to carry them.

Submersibles

S UBMERSIBLES ARE most easily defined as craft which use their ability to submerge to undertake their operations and protect them from detection and counter-attack. In general terms these are one-man operated weapons which have little autonomy other than that required for the immediate mission. They are of rough and sometimes ill-considered design, often produced quickly with little thought given to practicalities. Desperation resulting from a deteriorating military situation is often the prime motivating factor in their design, and they are usually as lethal to their operators as they are designed to be to the enemy. Unique to this field of naval operations are the suicide craft designed by the Japanese for use in the final months of the war.

The British *Welman*

Genesis of the design

The British organisation SOE (Special Operations Executive) was formally set up on 19 July 1940 and charged with co-ordinating 'all action by way of sub-

version and sabotage, against the enemy overseas'.[1] During the course of the Second World War SOE operated throughout Europe, the Middle East and the Far East with varying degrees of success. In doing so it established its own research and development department which produced a variety of weapons and other apparatus unavailable through more conventional channels. Research was carried out by SOE's Station IX at a former private hotel, The Fryth, near Welwyn Garden City in Hertfordshire while production was the responsibility of Station XII at Aston House near Stevenage. Some of their inventions like the 'S-Phone', a lightweight transceiver for agents in the field, were outstandingly successful: others such as the explosive turd[2] did little other than keep their inventors out of mischief. There was little attempt at co-ordination of research – individual projects and tastes were the order of the day

The *Welman* one-man midget submarine was the brainchild of the aptly named Colonel John Dolphin, an officer in the Royal Engineers, who envisaged the craft being used for attacks on enemy warships inside defended harbours, insertion of agents and stores

Lieutenant Jimmy Holmes RNVR sitting in the cockpit of a *Welman* one-man submersible. The photograph shows the cramped position for the operator with no means of observation save the ports cut into the 'conning tower'. Note the crude 'jumping wire' stays to allow the craft to slide under obstructions and the splash guard in front of the glass observation ports. (Author)

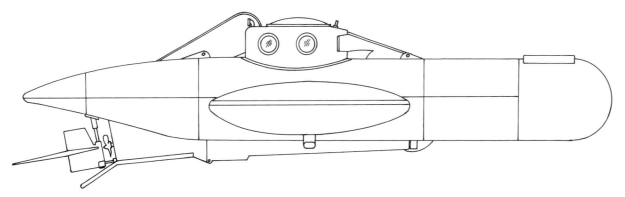

British *Welman* one-man submersible.

into enemy countries and beach reconnaissance. Development began at Welwyn (hence the name *Welman*: One Man Submarine made at Welwyn) in June and August 1942 and trials were carried out at Vickers' experimental tank at St Albans, the Admiralty experimental tank at Haslar, near Portsmouth, and also in Laleham Reservoir near Windsor.

Construction and machinery

It was indeed a curious craft which took to the water in January 1943 for preliminary trials. The first three *Welman*s were made at the Fryth and their construction reflected the amateurish nature of the operation.

Table 3: *Welman* technical particulars

DISPLACEMENT:	2.5 tons (with armament)
DIMENSIONS:	6.08m x 1.06m
PROPULSION:	One 2.5hp electric motor.
SPEED:	3kts (surfaced)
ENDURANCE:	36nm @ 3kts
ARMAMENT:	One 540kg explosive charge
CREW:	One

The *Welman* was a very simple craft, so simple that it represented the most that could be achieved with a minimum of resources and defied all attempts to improve it with what one operator has subsequently described as 'Thatcher-like arrogance'.[3] Externally, the craft was low-lying and of cylindrical appearance with a conning tower pierced by four armoured glass ports – no periscope was fitted – to enable the single operator to navigate the craft. Propulsion was by means of an electric motor, which came from a London bus, powered by a 40v battery of 220 amp/hrs capacity, although some early crafts' batteries were only 180 amp/hrs capacity. There were two ballast tanks, one port and one starboard, which were blown by compressed air but vented by a hand-operated lever. Submerged trim was maintained by a 300lb weight which had to be moved fore and aft as required by hand, although some later craft had proper compensating tanks and arrangements for trimming by pump. Diving depth was supposed to be 300ft but after a *Welman* imploded at 100ft while being lowered

on a measured wire during an unmanned test dive, orders were issued revising the maximum depth to which one of these craft could be taken.

The single operator sat amidships in a very cramped position on a seat salvaged from an Austin 7 car. He was supplied with oxygen via a face mask from a cylinder situated under the control panel but there was also a tray containing protosorb CO_2 absorption crystals. His controls were rudimentary in the extreme. A joy-stick, plundered from a Spitfire, governed the rudder and hydroplanes. There was only one set of hydroplanes, situated at the stern, which gave poor control when dived. This lack of control was shown in the *Welman*'s alarming tendency of porpoising at the slightest loss of trim. A foot-operated pump was provided for emptying the bilges and for the trimming tanks, where fitted. Other aids included a compass, barometer, ammeter, voltmeter and depth gauge.

The 'weapon' was a 540kg amatol charge secured to the fore end of the craft and held in position by rod gearing. The operator aimed to place his craft underneath the hull of the ship he was attacking. He would then release compressed air into the bow tank which forced the bow up so that the warhead was resting against the hull of the target. Magnets on the warhead would effectively hold the craft to the hull. The operator then released his craft from the warhead by means of the rod gearing which was first driven right home to arm the warhead before being unscrewed to achieve separation. During training it was found that the gearing was very stiff and separation could only be achieved after some fairly violent action by the operator which resulted in a lot of noise being made. At the same time the operator had to compensate for the loss of weight as a result of losing the warhead by shifting the trim weight forward by hand. A time fuse on the warhead would set the charge off 5 hours later by which time the *Welman* would be well clear, although it was fitted with various anti-tamper devices which would cause it to explode should it be discovered and an attempt made to remove or defuse it.

Attack instruments were basic in the extreme. A combined clock/stop-watch allowed the operator to time his run-in to the target using a Gyro Direction

A *Welman* submersible shown at the Fryth Hotel at Welwyn Garden City, where they were built and designed. (Author)

unclear how the craft were to be employed although strong interest was expressed by Admiral Louis Mountbatten, Chief of Combined Operations. Mountbatten even went so far as to 'drive' a *Welman* himself. Disaster nearly struck when one of the glass ports gave way when the craft was dived at 30ft and it was only by releasing the drop keel that Mountbatten was able to surface. After completion of the trials at Laleham, 150 *Welman*s were ordered on 23 February 1943: production was carried out at the Morris motor car factor at Cowley near Oxford. However, in October 1944 the order was reduced to 20, but production could not be stopped until 100 had been completed!

At this stage the *Welman*s seemed to have been earmarked for Combined Operations for use in beach reconnaissance. In the spring of 1943 the *Welman*s and their crews, who at this stage were largely drawn from No.2 Commando of the Royal Marines Special Boat Service, moved up to Scotland for more advanced training. Their first home was HMS *Titania*, a depot ship moored in Holy Loch. They then moved up to Lochgair were training in earnest started. After a few weeks the *Welman*s were transferred to HMS *Bonaventure*, another depot ship with special facilities for handling midget craft, and moved to Port HHX at Loch Cairnbrawn, a highly-secret establishment where the Royal Navy's midget submarines, X-Craft, and Chariots, were in training. While on the Clyde one *Welman*, *W.10*, was lost in a training accident – the hull was recovered in the 1960s.

It was here that the problem of how to get the *Welman* to the target area was addressed. Since the craft lacked sufficient endurance to make the journey unaided, it would have to be towed or carried there. Towing was out of the question since it would have been unbearable for the operator, but two methods of carrying the craft were evolved. In the first the *Welman* would be stowed on the upper casing of a submarine in the same way that the Royal Navy's Chariots were. A drawing in the Royal Navy Submarine Museum shows HMS *Thrasher*, a Group 2 'T' class submarine adapted for this purpose although it is not known whether she actually carried *Welman*s on exercises. The alternative was to carry the *Welman* slung in the davits of a destroyer or MTB. The possibility of towing the *Welman*, while mounted in a 'skid' at high speed from an MTB was also investigated but not pursued very far – probably to the great relief of those manning the craft!

Indicator, also salvaged from a Spitfire, set by eye to maintain the correct course. Since the operator was not provided with a periscope he had to approach his target either by running awash with the conning tower just above the water or by approaching the target dived while 'porpoising' frequently, but briefly, to check the course. Harvey Bennette was a Sub-Lieutenant stationed at the Fryth who was involved with the Welman project. He recalled that:

> The whole business of having no periscope, which made the craft blind, was something no-one could understand. No one came to appreciate why there was no periscope – the lack of such an instrument made the things unusable because they were blind.[4]

Bennette ascribed this astonishing omission to the all-pervasive influence of Colonel Dolphin on the project. He was the banyan tree under whose shade nothing else would grow. The *Welman* was very much his idea and all outside suggestions were stoutly resisted. It is clear that the operator would be a very busy man during an attack and this was one of the greatest flaws of the design. In fact, other than having an engine and marginally better instrumentation, the operator's position was little different to that of Ezra Lee in his *Turtle* in 1776. There was simply too much for one man to do for the craft to be effective. Moreover, by making it a one-man craft the designers denied the operator the moral support which would come from another member of the crew.

Training

Training in the *Welman*s was carried out initially at Laleham Reservoir near Windsor. At this stage it was

Welman operations

In the autumn of 1943 – the date is uncertain – Combined Operations decided that the *Welman* was not suited to their purposes. The decision was probably taken after General Sir Robin Laycock took over Combined Operations after Mountbatten's departure for better things in India as Supreme Allied Commander. Laycock, a professional soldier, clearly had no use for the *Welman*s which had so obviously appealed to Mountbatten. The SBS personnel were redeployed and the Admiralty found itself the unwilling custodian of these craft. However, Admiral Sir Lionel Wells KCB DSO, Flag Officer commanding Orkney and Shetlands, got to hear of them and thought that they would be useful for attacks on German shipping using coastal waters inside the Leads off Norway. MTBs of the 30th (later 54th) Flotilla, operating from Lerwick and manned by officers and men of the Royal Norwegian Navy, were already engaged in these operations but it was thought that the *Welman*s would be a useful addition to the forces available. They would be carried over to the Leads, the strip of water between the outer islands and the Norwegian mainland, by the MTBs which would select a suitable place to hide, usually an uninhabited island. An observation post would be established and the crews would wait until a suitable target presented itself. The *Welman* was used only once in operations. On 21 November 1943 four 'Welmen' were towed to a position off Bergen in Norway with orders to attack the large Laskevag floating dock which the Germans were making increased use of for U-boat repairs. The operation was a failure. One craft was captured and the operators of the remaining three scuttled their craft and 'headed for the hills' (literally) to await recovery by a Norwegian MTB. The *Welman*'s operational career was over. On 15 February 1944 Laycock formally notified the Admiralty that Combined Operations had no further use for these craft. Rear-Admiral (Submarines), Rear-Admiral Claude Barry, agreed and ordered no further use be found for them.

The *Welman* concept enjoyed a brief revival with the *Welfreighter*, a four-man submersible which could carry up to 2 tons of stores. It was originally intended to use these craft in the Adriatic, taking supplies to Albanian partisans but the war ended before they could be deployed. Instead eight *Welfreighter*s went to the Far East, based at Port Moresby. From there they would take supplies, towed part of the way by 66ft-'Snake' class sailing ketches, to the Malay Peninsula where a guerrilla war was in progress against the Japanese. But here too, the war ended before they could be deployed. After the war the remaining craft were simply abandoned, broken up in the great post-war disposal of naval and military equipment declared surplus to requirements. One survives at the Royal Navy Submarine Museum at Gosport.

The German *Neger/Marder*

German submersibles were among the most impractical and lethal (to their operators) designs of any produced by the belligerents during the Second World War. Despite the fact that, as latecomers to this field,

they had the experience of their Italian and Japanese allies to draw on, they profited little from it.

Admiral Heye was under no illusions about the magnitude of the task facing him:

> We ourselves possessed no practical experience in this form of warfare. We knew broadly that the Italians and the British possessed several different forms of small battle weapons, but we knew nothing of the Japanese operations with midget submarines.[5]

Although Heye had what amounted to a licence to organise his own production programme, he was handicapped by two restrictions. Firstly, Donitz would not let him have any men from the U-boat arm and therefore Heye would have to scrape his men from other sections of the *Wehrmacht*.[6] Heye recruited from all three of the German armed forces and apparently was not particularly choosy about where his men came from. Lieutenant Richard Hale RNVR of the minesweeper HMS *Orestes* recalled the interrogation of a *Marder* operator captured on 8 July 1945 during operations off Normandy:

> . . . the prisoner turned out to be eighteen years old who had been in cells for some crime and had been let out to do his suicide job.[7]

Secondly, the need to produce the new weapons as quickly as possible meant that there would be little time for research and development. The new craft would have to be built from components of existing craft or weapons.

Conception and design

Speed and expediency were the two factors which dominated German construction of these weapons. Admiral Heye later commented:

> As speed was essential there was no question of lengthy tests and trials. At my suggestion the Commander-in-Chief gave me considerable powers which enabled me to short circuit tedious bureaucratic procedure and to have direct contact to have direct contact with all departments of the Naval Staff and – especially important – with industrial concerns. Unless I had made full use of these powers, the formation and equipment of the *K-force* would hardly have been feasible in the short time available.[8]

The *Welman* may have been a faintly Heath-Robinson contraption but the three German submersibles were lethal to their operators. If there was a philosophy behind their design it was simply to produce a torpedo carrier that could be built cheaply and in large numbers to overwhelm an Allied invasion fleet. The first such German weapon was based on the standard G7e torpedo, designed by *Stabsingenieur* Mohr and developed at the *Torpedo Versuchs Anstalt* (TVA) at

German *Neger* one-man submersible.

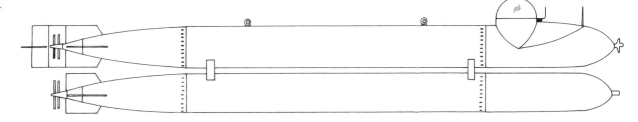

A *Neger* beached at Anzio in April 1944, the operator having suffocated. This was the fate which befell most *Neger* operators. The operator sat in an extremely cramped position and was too low down to see the target properly – the merest oil slick on the water would foul the perspex canopy. The spike at the forward end of the craft is the aiming spike which together with a graduated scale engraved on the canopy constituted his sole fire-control instrument. (Imperial War Museum: NA 14029)

Eckenforde near Kiel. Mohr played a considerable part in the development of the craft, including doing much of the testing, that the name given to the craft, *Neger* ('Nigger') was a pun on his own name (*Mohr* is the German for 'Moor'). The weapon was extremely simple and consisted of a G7e torpedo which had been fitted with a small cockpit covered with a plexiglass dome for the single operator to sit in.

The craft was powered by an electric motor similar to that used in the conventional torpedo. It weighed some 5 tonnes and had a range of 30nm at 3kts. It was armed with a single G7e torpedo which was slung underneath it.

Table 4: *Neger/Marder* technical particulars

DISPLACEMENT:	2.7 tons
DIMENSIONS:	7.6m x 0.5m
PROPULSION:	Single shaft, one 12hp electric motor
SPEED:	4kts
ENDURANCE:	48nm @ 3 knots
ARMAMENT:	One G7e electric torpedo.
CREW:	One

The craft could not dive but possessed merely sufficient positive buoyancy to support the torpedo. A larger version of *Neger* called *Marder* was built which

incorporated a diving tank and could dive to a depth of 25m for very short periods.

The operator was provided with rudimentary controls, a wrist compass, a self-contained Draeger breathing set and a crude aiming device consisting of a graduated scale marked on the perspex dome and an aiming spike on the 'nose' of the craft rather like the foresight on a rifle. A handle in the cockpit released the torpedo which started and ran at a preset depth. One disadvantage of the craft was that on occasions the torpedo started but failed to release, carrying the upper unit and operator to oblivion.

In theory, and especially in the eyes of the shore-based planners, the vision of a swarm of *Marder* overwhelming an invasion fleet was an attractive one. In reality the position was very different. The operator was too low to see properly and the perspex dome was easily obscured by oil or other scum in the water rendering the operator blind. If he opened the perspex lid to get a better view, he risked swamping the craft. The casualty rate of between 60 to 80 per cent suffered by *Neger/Marder* crew on operations was a direct result of these design faults. Some 200 *Neger* and 300 *Marder* were delivered. Of the *Neger*s some 120 were lost in action – the numbers of *Marder* lost is unclear.

Neger/Marder operations

*Neger*s/*Marder*s were not so much deployed as flung at the Anglo-American invasion fleets off Anzio and the Normandy beaches. In theory these operational areas offered a multiplicity of targets in the shape of Allied warships and transports anchored off the beaches, but in practice the operations were nothing short of disastrous. The shortcomings of the design became obvious when it was found that owing to the shallow gradient of the beaches at Anzio, the *Neger* operators had to conscript 500 unwilling soldiers to dig launching ramps. Their sole operation at Anzio was on the night of 20/21 April 1944 when twenty-four *Neger* were despatched against the invasion fleet. Thirteen returned having been unable to find a target while at least four were sunk by the escorts. One *Neger* was washed up on the beach, with the operator dead in the cockpit – thus providing an example of this new weapon for the Allies to study. The remaining five craft simply disappeared and presumably were lost in accidents. No Allied ships were reported as sunk or damaged. It was an ominous portent for the future.

Normandy was the next target for the *Marder* operators. Here their operations were even more circumscribed by their environment than at Anzio. Because of overwhelming Allied air superiority the *Marder* had to be launched at night, and then needed the ebb tide to help them reach their targets. They would attack their targets and, hopefully, return to shore with the flood tide. These constraints effectively restricted *Marder* operations to only three or four nights per month.

Despite the fact that a *Neger* had been captured intact at Anzio, the appearance of its half-sister off Normandy on the night of 5/6 July 1944 came as something as a surprise. The Allies had already adopted a plan for the defence of the invasion anchorage. Owing to the restrictions placed on the movement of German ships and U-boats by their own minefields and by the overwhelming Allied air superiority, static defence was adopted. It reduced the risk of collision and kept wear and tear on ships' hulls and machinery to a minimum. Seaward patrols under the command of Captain A F Pugsley RN and consisted of a line of minesweepers anchored 5 cables[9] apart, 6 miles from the shore and parallel to it. The minesweepers were backed up by two or three divisions of MTBs and by a number of destroyers.

Defence from attacks launched from seaward was not really a problem. The real threat came from attacks launched from the land, and in particular from the eastern section of the assault area. There was little threat to the American anchorages in the western section of the assault area following the swift American occupation of the eastern coast of the Cotentin peninsula. On the other hand in the eastern section, the Germans were still holding the ground to the east of the River Orne in strength together with the port of Le Havre and it was from this area that the main threat would come. The defence of the eastern anchorages called for vigorous measures, and it was decided that the current static patrols be strengthened by the formation of the Support Squadron Eastern Flank under the command of Commander K A Sellar RN. The squadron consisted of the old China gunboat HMS *Locust* as headquarters ship and seventy-one other craft, mostly LCGs, LCFs, LCSs and Motor Launches manned by a total of 240 officers and 3000 men.

A double patrol line was established running roughly 6 miles to the north of Ouistreham and from there for 2 miles in a north westerly direction until it entered the area where the seaward defence patrols were operating. The first line consisted of the landing craft, anchored 3½ cables apart. The second line consisted of one motor launch to every two craft in the static line. If things were quiet then the MLs simply secured to one of the landing craft. On an alert being sounded, they cast off and patrolled the area between the two craft for which they were responsible. This system was known as the *Trout Line*. The nightly deployment of the *Trout Line* was a matter of extremely accurate timing. If the line was deployed too early, then the ships would be shelled from the shore. Retirement in the morning had to be done just before first light for the same reason. The *Trout Line* was first deployed on 28 June and from then until the night of 5 July, it enjoyed a quiet existence.

The first sighting of a *Marder* came as somewhat of

German *Molch* one-man submersible.

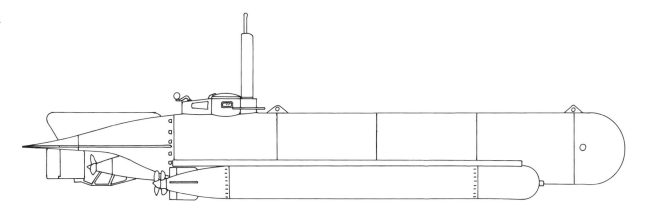

a surprise. The experience of *ML.151* may be taken as typical of that of the ships of the Support Squadron that morning. *ML.151* was moored astern of *LCF.21* in the static defence line when, shortly after 3.00am, her attention was called by loudhailer to an object moving on the landing craft's starboard quarter. *ML.151* went astern but at 3.07am a torpedo passed under her and headed off in the direction of *LCG(L).681*. The ML then tried to ram but was forced to turn away on account of gunfire from *LCF.21* and *LCG(M).681*. At 3.15am the enemy dived and *ML.151* plastered the area with 5lb scuttling charges before proceeding to drop similar charges over a much larger area east of the *Trout Line*. This engagement set the pattern for many that night and early the next morning. The British were not at all sure at what they were firing at and it was not until the morning when the night's results could be collated and the prisoners taken interrogated, that some kind of sense could be made of what had happened. Thirteen of the weapons had been destroyed and a number of their operators taken prisoner. However, on the debit side was the loss of the minesweepers HMS *Magic* and *Cato*.

Further *Marder* sorties were launched on 8/9 July, 2/3 August, 15/16 August and 17 August. The operations were extremely unsuccessful: in return for the loss of ninety-nine *Marder* the losses inflicted on the British amounted to one destroyer, three minesweepers, a trawler, two merchant ships and a number of landing craft – in an area packed with transports and warships. The lack of any significant successes reflects on the unsuitability of the *Marder* as an attack weapon. The craft may have technically reliable but the single operator was hopelessly overworked. He had to conn his craft, sneak past an alert and aggressive defence and then select a target while sitting in an extremely uncomfortable position and only able to see a few inches above the water, the surface of which would have been fouled by oil and other detritus. Most of the *Marder* operators probably fired at the first shadow that loomed up before them. They were never employed operationally again.

The German *Molch*

Conception and design

A successor to the *Neger/Marder* combination was the *Molch* (Salamander). This was basically nothing more than a slug-like craft which was a carrier for G7e torpedoes slung externally on either side of the craft. As with other German designs it was designed to use as many existing components as possible. The craft can be divided into two sections. The fore section contained the battery. The size of the battery meant that the *Molch* was a comparatively large craft with an impressive underwater range – although whether the single operator could stand such a voyage was another matter.

Table 5: *Molch* technical particulars

DISPLACEMENT:	11 tons
DIMENSIONS:	10.8m x 1.8m
PROPULSION:	Single shaft, one 13hp motor powered by twelve Type 13 T210 battery troughs
SPEED:	4.3kts (surfaced), 5kts (dived)
ENDURANCE:	50nm @ 4kts (surface), 50nm @ 5kts (dived)
ARMAMENT:	Two G7e electric torpedoes.
CREW:	One

Behind the battery in the after section was the operator's position. He sat between two trimming tanks whose relatively small size and position must have made them almost useless in compensating for the weight of the battery. In fact when the first production model went out on trials, it proved impossible to make her submerge and therefore most *Molch* operations were carried out with the craft running awash. Therefore a simple design fault robbed the *Molch* of its most important asset – concealment. The controls were extremely simple. A magnetic compass was fitted externally although in some boats an automatic pilot was installed together with a simple hydrophone. A periscope was fitted but its use was negated by the fact that it could only be rotated 30° either side of the centre line. Finally behind the operator was the electric motor.

Despite the problems associated with the *Molch*'s handling, series production was begun in June 1944 with a total of 393 units being completed by the end of February 1945. Production was largely centred at the works of Deschimag AG Weser at Bremen.

Molch operations

Molch were deployed to Norway, Heligoland, the Low Countries and Southern France although actual operations were confined to the Schedlt Estuary in the bitter winter of 1944-45. Generally they were held in reserve since the *Biber*, considered a superior craft, was also operating in the same area. Any chance for success in this theatre was removed on 3 February 1945 when the *Molch* depot at Poortershavn was virtually destroyed in an air raid by 617 Squadron.

The German *Biber*

Conception and design

An altogether different creature was the *Biber* one-man submersible whose development arose from the capture of *Welman 46* at Bergen on 22 November 1943. The *Welman* was of dubious operational value, as we have seen, but the *Kriegsmarine* fell upon this specimen as if it were gift from heaven. In particular the *Welman* acted as a spur to *Korvettenkapitän* Hans Bartels to develop something similar. The Germans inspected *W.46* in minute detail noting that 'The enemy continues the mini-war with ever new ideas'.[10] In a service not known for eccentrics, Bartels stood out like a beacon in the stuffy world of the

Kriegsmarine. During the 1940 Norwegian campaign he had taken the surrender of a Norwegian destroyer and an entire flotilla of torpedo-boats. He then designed and built a minesweeper to his own specification, followed by eleven more, and then invited OKM to pay for them. When Grand Admiral Erich Raeder indignantly refused, Bartels moored one of the minesweepers in a canal opposite German naval headquarters in Berlin where Raeder could inspect the craft. Raeder took a dim view of these proceedings and Bartels was packed off to the destroyer *Z-34* to cool his heels in the 'real' navy.

Bartels evidently found considerable inspiration in the *Welman* and on 4 February 1944 he began negotiations with Flenderwek of Lubeck for the construction of a similar craft. On 15 March 1944 the first pro-

A *Molch* running awash. The tremendous length of the craft was dictated by the size of the battery. The operator sat at the aft end of the craft. (Author)

A German *Biber* submersible photographed in the Baltic in 1945. The 'thatch' around the periscope is designed to conceal the tell-tale 'feather' when the craft was operating close inshore or in rivers. (Author)

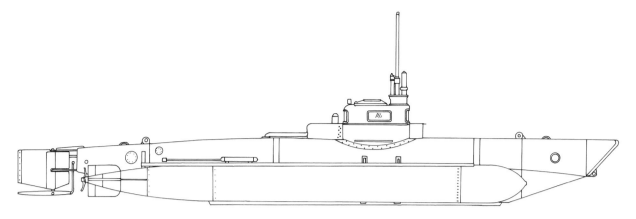

German *Biber* one-man submersible.

totype, known as either the *Bunte-Boot* (after Director Bunte of Flenderwerke) or *Adam*, was complete. Trials, with Bartels doing much of the testing, were run on the River Trave and on 29 March 1944 the craft was formally accepted for service. Twenty-four production models were ordered as a first batch out of an eventual production run of 324. Deliveries throughout 1944 were as follows: May (3); June (6); July (19); August (50); September (117); October (73); November (56). Although air raids on Kiel destroyed some components, Allied bombing failed to disrupt production to any appreciable degree.

Table 6: *Biber* technical particulars

DISPLACEMENT:	6.3 tons
DIMENSIONS:	9m x 1.6m
PROPULSION:	Single shaft, one 32hp Opel-blitz Otto petrol engine. One 13hp electric motor from electric torpedo powered by three Type T13 T210 battery troughs
FUEL CAPACITY:	0.11 tons
SPEED:	6.5kts (surfaced), 5.3kts (submerged)
ENDURANCE:	130nm @ 6kts (surfaced), 8.6nm @ 5kts (submerged)
ARMAMENT:	Two G7e electric torpedoes.
CREW:	One

The exhaust system of the *Biber* was less than satisfactory. This photograph shows *Biber 90* in the tow of HMS *Ready*'s motor boat on 29 December 1944. The craft had been found drifting on the surface with the operator dead in his seat, overcome by petrol fumes. (Author)

Reservations had been expressed about the safety of a petrol motor in such a small craft but these were dismissed by Dr Bunte. Petrol engines were cheap to make and could be supplied in quantity, and as an added advantage they made very little noise when running. However, the reservations were well founded. Like all petrol engines the Opel-Blitz in the *Biber* gave off carbon monoxide in its exhaust. Thus the operator sat in a potentially lethal atmosphere if he ran the engine for any longer than 45 minutes with the upper hatch shut. When the Royal Navy examined *Biber 90*, captured intact by HMS *Ready* on 29 December 1944 (the operator having suffocated in the 'cabin'), they noted that 'The atmosphere inside the boat was heavy with a mixture of petrol vapour, oxygen and battery gas'.[11] Operators were supplied with breathing apparatus and 20 hours worth of oxygen but many must have succumbed to CO poisoning while on operations.

The hull was made of 3mm sheet steel and gave a safe diving depth of 60ft although some *Biber* went down to over 100ft on operations. Four internal bulkheads and three longitudinal ribs reinforced the hull plating. There were no compensating or trimming tanks, just a single diving tank in the bow and another in the stern. The *Biber* handled well on the surface but it proved virtually impossible to control when dived – largely owing to the lack of any trimming arrangements. As the British inspectors reported:

> Even allowing for the fact that she is strange to us, the boat is certainly extremely 'tender'. In a static trim dive she quickly took up angles of 40° bows up and bows down. This inherent longitudinal tenderness is accentuated by the effects of the free surfaces in the main ballast tanks and the petrol tank.[12]

The *Biber* was built in three sections which bolted together. The bow section contained nothing more than the main diving tank. Between the first and second bulkhead was the main compartment where the operator sat with his head poking up into the 28in conning tower. The control panel was directly in front of the operator's seat and was compact and aus-

The conning tower of *Biber 55* with the hatch open. The three masts are, from forward to aft, the container for the magnetic compass, the non-revolving forward facing periscope and the air induction mast. Behind the conning tower is the exhaust pipe, tank and valve from the petrol engine. (Author)

The operator's position in a *Biber*, reflecting the austere and rudimentary nature of the design. The 'helm' is in the centre with the rudder indicator on the lower left and hydroplane indicator on the lower right. Above, from left to right, are the indicators for engine oil pressure, oxygen pressure and battery voltage, LP air and HP air. The depth gauge is upper left. The three armoured glass ports are also visible. (Imperial War Museum: MH 29893)

from the engine was vented outboard but British inspectors found that:

> The muffler valve on the exhaust trunking was regarded as a poor and unreliable piece of work, so designed that the slightest amount of carbon on the seating would cause a failure and the flooding of the main engine.[13]

The final compartment in the boat contained the after diving tank. There were no facilities for the operator whatsoever. He was given a ration of chocolate which had been 'improved' with the addition of stimulants such as caffeine and kola but that was his lot.

Two G7e torpedoes were slung on a rail in semi-recessed positions on either side of the craft. The torpedoes were clamped to the rail which ran from a fitting on the keel to a swinging eyebolt above the rail. Above the rail was a pneumatic cylinder to which air was admitted in order to fire the torpedo. The piston in the cylinder then travelled toward the rear, releasing a clamping eyebolt and forcing back a trip lever on the torpedo, which then started and ran forward under its own power suspended from the rail by two lugs until it cleared the submarine. The firing arrangements were, if anything, too simple and there were to be two serious incidents of 'negligent discharge' in which a number of craft were wrecked and their operators killed. An alternative armament to the torpedoes was the mine. Two GS mines could be carried by each craft. The mines were fitted with either magnetic/acoustic or magnetic/pressure fuses.

Biber operations

Biber made their operation debut in Normandy from the end of August 1944 in a singularly unsuccessful fashion. It had been intended for them to operate from Le Havre, but the town fell to Anglo-American forces on 20 August. Undaunted, the *K-Flotille 261* pressed on – it took them 5 days to make the journey from their depot in Belgium to the port of Fecamp, which was to be their new base, where they arrived on 28 August. Eighteen *Biber* were launched on the night of 29/30 August – less than 24 hours after they had arrived. In contrast to the *Neger* missions, all eighteen returned. However, there is not even the most oblique reference to the attack in the official British narratives. On 31 August *K-Flotille 261* was forced to abandon Fecamp in the face of the Allied advance. Those *Biber* which were left behind were wrecked and the few which were taken away were subsequently destroyed in a night action with an Allied armoured column and this episode marked the end of *K-Verband* operations in Normandy.

Between the beginning of September and the beginning of December there was little in the way of *K-Verband* operations, largely due to the shifting

A view looking aft inside a captured *Biber* which had been dismantled by the British. This section would normally contain the batteries which have been removed. (Author)

tere. The conning tower was fitted with glass ports which were the operator's principle means of seeing where he was going. A periscope was fitted but it was fixed facing forward. Maintaining the craft at periscope depth was almost impossible because of the lack of trimming arrangements. Behind the operator was the compartment containing the engine. British inspectors noticed that it was almost impossible to access the engine for routine maintenance without parting the craft. In theory this was sealed off from the main compartment but in practice the insidious petrol vapour permeated every part of the boat. Exhaust

nature of the front making it difficult to establish an operating base with any degree of security. However, the planners were not short of ideas for the future employment of their craft. The Channel Islands were suggested as a suitable base, but the idea was soon dropped when it was realised that the craft would have to be transported to the Channel Islands by air using large slow transport aircraft and with the prospect of horrific losses in the face of Allied air superiority. Moreover, the prospect of the small and unseaworthy *Marder* and *Biber* having to cope with the notorious tides and races around the Channel Islands did not bear thinking about.

From mid-December 1944 until the end of the war *Biber* operations were concentrated in the Scheldt estuary. This area appeared to be very promising. There were numerous inlets and islands amongst which the *K-Verband* could be hidden and the growing use of the port of Antwerp meant that there would be no shortage of targets, and the German Navy's *B-Dienst* station on the island of Schouwen was in an excellent position to report shipping movements. However, operations would be strongly constrained by weather conditions and the state of the tide. For their survival *Biber* required wind and sea states of less than State Four on the Beaufort Scale: anything greater and they would be swamped. Secondly, there should no moon. The *Biber* would sail on the ebb tide so that the 40 or so miles to the western Scheldt would be covered fairly quickly so they would arrive in the operational area at dusk. The wholly inadequate periscope fitted in the *Biber* meant that periscope attacks at night were impossible, forcing them to attack on the surface.

An advanced base was prepared at Poortershavn and Heelevoetsluis at the head of the Waal/Maas estuary. The main base was Rotterdam where thirty *Biber* and thirty *Molch* were sent. The *Biber* would be towed down from Rotterdam by units of the Rhine Flotilla to Hellevoetsluis where their tows would be slipped and the craft would proceed independently. A further sixty *Molch* would arrive at Assens from Helgoland together with thirty *Biber* from Groningen. A further sixty *Biber* would arrive in the area in January 1945.

But all this concentration of force achieved little. Eighteen *Biber* sailed from Poortershavn and Hellevoetsluis on the night of 22/23 December 1944. The operation ended in failure when British MTBs surprised the *Biber* while their tows were being slipped and four were lost instantly. One was mined and one returned damaged. The remaining twelve disappeared. No cause has ever been given for their loss but suffocation from petrol fumes and accidental flooding while proceeding on the surface are the most likely reasons. Only one success was recorded and that was the sinking of the 4700-ton *Alan a Dale*.

This operation set the tone for four months of sustained operations by *K-Verband* in the Low Countries. Night after night *Biber* and *Molch* would be launched against Allied shipping for no result and with most of the craft failing to return. Grand-Admiral Karl Donitz, Commander-in-Chief of the *Kriegsmarine*, referred to the operators as *Opferkampfer* (suicide fighters). It says much for the morale of the *K-Verband* that they were prepared to continue with these operations in the almost certain knowledge that they would not return. By the end of 1944 thirty-one *Biber* had been lost in return for one merchant ship sunk. This was hardly an inspiring exchange rate. Only eight of the *Biber* lost were claimed by the Allies, the rest as a result of operator error or accident. On 27 December a force of fourteen *Biber* was preparing to sail from Hellevoetsluis when two G7 torpedoes were accidentally fired into the lock. In the resulting conflagration eleven of the *Biber* were destroyed together with two launches. Undeterred the three remaining craft set out. This dismal record convinced many in the *Kriegsmarine* that *K-Verband* operations were a waste of resources and manpower. But Donitz disagreed. He had great hopes for the *Biber* particularly in its role as a minelayer and in the two-man *Seehund* midget submarines which were just coming into production. However as the Flag Officer Channel Coast cryptically remarked, since no-one had yet returned from a *Biber* operation, their success could not be guaranteed![14] The figures for January and February 1945 were not better. Sixteen out of twenty-nine *Biber* deployed were sunk for no losses in allied shipping. On 6 March there was another torpedo accident at Heelevoetsluis when a torpedo was accidentally fired in the basin at Rotterdam. Fourteen *Biber* were sunk and nine more damaged. Operational losses in March were equally appalling: forty-two out of fifty-six *Biber* for no result.[15] In April 1945 there were four more operations in April which involved a total of twenty-four *Biber* and in which nineteen were lost. No Allied vessels were sunk or damaged in these operations.

The *K-Verband* operations in the Low Countries were characterised by considerable bravery and endurance by the *K-Manner* but set against a singular lack of success. The reasons are this are legion. Poor equipment and inadequate training account for some of the failures. Other factors include bad weather and very aggressive opponents who possessed overwhelming *materiel* superiority and who enjoyed complete command of the air. However, the Germans did develop three operations for the *Biber* which, although they were either unsuccessful or never implemented, remain of interest to the historian. A most adventurous plan was for the employment of a *Biber* in the Suez Canal.[16] In an operation similar to Italian and British ideas, the *Biber* would be loaded into a Bv.222 flying-boat (the aircraft would require

A *Biber* abandoned on the beach at Fecamp in Normandy in August 1944. The photograph gives a good view of the recesses in the hull where the armament of two G7e torpedoes would be carried. An alternative armament was mines – the *Bibers* might have been more successful if employed exclusively as covert minelayers. (Author)

substantial modification) and landed on the Great Bitter Lakes in the Suez Canal. The *Biber* would then be released with the intention of sinking a ship and blocking the canal. The plan was ingenious but hopelessly impractical. The Bv.222 was the largest operational flying boat in the world with a wingspan of 46m. Its arrival over the Suez Canal would hardly be a low-key affair. The plan never went beyond the most preliminary of planning stages.

Another use for the *Biber* was an abortive attempt to destroy the road bridge over the river Waal at Nijmegen which had been captured by the US 82nd Airborne Division in September 1944. Assault frogmen had already made an unsuccessful but daring raid on the rail bridge. After this incident the defences around the bridges were strengthened by rigging four net barriers across the Waal upstream from the bridge. The operation began on the night of 12/13 January 1945 when the Germans released 240 mines in four waves. These were to destroy the net barriers and were followed by twenty *Biber*, each with their periscopes camouflaged to resemble floating nests. These were to fire torpedoes fitted with hooks to catch the nets and blow gaps in them. Finally four more *Biber* towed 600lb explosive charges which would be released to drift down under the bridge. Each charge was fitted with a photo-electric cell. As the charge floated under the bridge the change of light would trigger the charge and complete the night's work of destruction. But the operation was a failure. Both banks of the Waal were held in strength by the Allies and after the explosion of the mines, the river was raked by gunfire, destroying all four of the explosive charges before they passed the net barriers.

The most serious attempt to use the *Biber* in a major operation was a plan to attack the Soviet battleship *Archangelsk* at her moorings in the Kola Inlet. *K-flotilla 265* was formed and despatched to Harstadt in Norway for this very purpose in November 1944, although actual planning for the operation had started some time earlier. Like the Japanese, British and Italians the Germans planned to deliver the *Biber* to the operational area by carrying them on the casing of selected U-boats. Trials had already taken place in the Baltic and the method found to work. However, the Germans failed to learn from the experience of their Allies in one respect. The Italians had always carried their *Maiale* in containers secured to the casing to protect the craft from weather damage and, to a certain extent, insulate them from the vibration of the parent submarine's machinery. The *Kriegsmarine* took no such precautions, the *Biber* travelling on simple chocks mounted on the casing, directly above two large, throbbing diesels in the U-boat's engine-room.

As might be expected German preparations were thorough. There was plenty of aerial reconnaissance material available of the area but in order to obtain precise information, arrangements were made to capture some local fishermen whose subsequent interrogation provided a good deal of information on the defences in the Kola Inlet. The defences were formidable and consisted mainly of patrols by local anti-submarine craft. The bay itself was protected by a net and boom on each side of the island at Salny. The date for the operation hinged on the state of the moon. The planners wanted sufficient moonlight to give the operators a sight of their target without necessarily exposing them to discovery. On 8 January 1945, the date favoured by the planners, the tables showed that a half moon would rise at midnight and would still provide enough light by 3.00am. This was reckoned sufficient to allow the *Biber* to make their run-in and carry out the attack.

The plan was for the U-boats to leave Harstadt on X–3 and to launch the *Biber* at X–12 hours when 40 miles from the enemy anchorage. Thus the *Biber* would have 12 hours in order to get into position–not long given their underwater speed. Following the attack a rendezvous was arranged to seaward of Sjet Navolok. The *Biber* were to lie on the bottom and make contact with their parent U-boat by SST. The craft would then be abandoned and scuttled, the operators being recovered to the parent boat. An alternative rendezvous was arranged for X + 1 off the Fischer peninsula. This would have been the more likely pick-up point for the planners had allowed the *Biber* 12 hours to approach the target but only 4 hours to get out. Any operator who missed both rendezvous was instructed to make for Persfjord, ditch his craft and head for Sweden on foot.

Accordingly the three U-boats, *U-295*, *U-318* and *U-716*, departed from Harstadt on 5 January making most of the running on the surface. This was the operation's undoing. In a periodic inspection it was found that in two of the *Biber* the vibration had caused leaks in the petrol pipes. This was easily put right by the U-boat's engineering department and the submarines continued, albeit at a slower speed. But a subsequent examination of the *Biber* when the force was off the North Cape showed that further leaks in the petrol pipes had developed together with leaks in the stern glands. As a result water had entered the machinery space in some of the craft. Reluctantly the operation was cancelled and the force returned to Harstadt. Had the attack gone in on 8 January then the *Biber* operators would have found the anchorage deserted barring local defence craft. Convoy RA-62 had sailed on 10 December 1944 and the next convoy, JW-63, would not arrive until the evening of 8 January. *Arkhangelsk* herself was safely in the White Sea.

The only other area where *K-Verband* craft were employed was the Mediterranean where a number of *Marder* and *Molch* units participated in attacks on Allied shipping off Villefranche at the end of 1944. No successes were achieved and the operations of the *K-Verband* were hopelessly compromised by the confused political situation operating in that theatre at the time.

In one respect operations by *Neger/Marder*, *Molch*

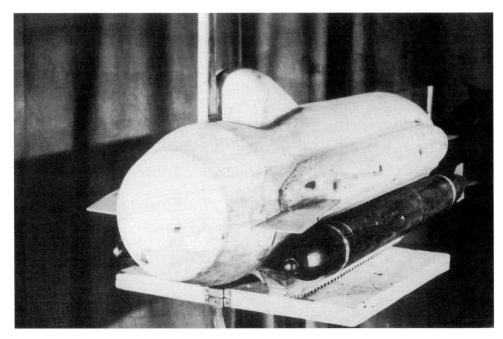

A model of the proposed *Seeteufel* submersible, which was to be fitted with caterpillar tracks to allow it to make its own way into the water. (Author)

and *Biber* exceeded their designers' wildest dreams. These simple and ill-conceived craft were given a far higher capability by the British than their operational successes warranted. Expensive and unwelcome precautions had to be taken to deal with them. At a conservative estimate some 500 British ships and over 1000 Fleet Air Arm and RAF aircraft were specifically tasked with anti-midget submarine operations from June 1944 until the end of the war. In a sense they acted as a traditional 'fleet in being', tying down a large number of enemy forces. But this was not their designed function.

Seeteufel and other German designs

Further developments of the *Biber* were planned which included two-man versions, the *Biber II* and *Biber III*. However, these were nothing more than drawing-board projects. Their cancellation was as a result of a directive issued by OKM at the beginning of 1945 to the effect that work on all craft not in series production should be suspended. But this directive was largely ignored. The fact that Admiral Heye was virtually independent of the *Kriegsmarine*'s command structure ensured that work proceeded on a number of designs until the end of the war. Among the most ingenious of these designs was for the *Seeteufel* (Sea Devil) which was an amphibious craft fitted with both a single propeller and caterpillar tracks. The requirement for a tracked craft arose from the difficulties experienced in launching *Marder* and *Molch* without dockside facilities. The *Seeteufel* could simply make its own way into the water.

As built the prototype had a two-man crew and was much larger than other midget types. Propulsion was by either a 80hp petrol engine which could be switched to drive either the single screw or the caterpillar tracks. For submerged drive the boat had a 25hp electric motor giving a speed of 8kts which was very good considering that the *Seeteufel* had the worst underwater resistance of any German midget sub. The petrol engine was installed in the bow beneath a fixed schnorckel mast which also contained the periscope, a rod aerial and the magnetic compass with lighting transmission. Behind the petrol engine was the crew compartment. All controls were grouped into an aircraft-like control column placed forward of the driver's seat beneath a plexiglass dome. Despite the fat shape of the boat, *Seeteufel* handled well under water. The diving depth was 21m. Tests on the craft proved satisfactory except that it was found that on land the engine lacked power and the tracks were too narrow. In the water, however, the craft handled perfectly well. Heye was impressed and entered into negotiations with the automobile manufacturers Carl Borgward for series production of the *Seeteufel* with a more powerful 250hp diesel engine. But these plans came to nothing, and the prototype was taken to Lubeck where it was destroyed at the end of the war.

Other designs investigated but not put into series production included the *Delphin*, a small streamlined craft which towed a 500kg mine. The craft was quite fast with an underwater speed of 14kts powered by a 2.5-litre Opel-Kapitan closed-cycle engine. Only two craft were built and trials showed some promise. But both were destroyed at Potenitz on 1 May 1945 to prevent their falling into the hands of the British. Another craft was *Schwertal*, a two-man craft armed with two torpedoes which bore an uncomfortable resemblance to the Japanese *Kaiten*. It was a development of the Type XXVIIF U-boat whose construction had been halted at the end of 1944. The Type XXVIIF was powered by a closed-cycle Walther Turbine and could achieve a underwater speed of 20.4ks with torpedoes slung and 20kts unarmed. The use of the closed-cycle drive conferred numerous advantages, including high speed and the ability to dispense with separate systems for surface and submerged drive.

Schwertal was to be a fast and manoeuvrable underwater craft and was intended to have an ASW role as

well as an anti-shipping one. She was to be armed with two torpedoes but other suggested weapons included the 500kg towed mine and underwater rockets for use against pursuing ships. The high speed of the craft meant that she could not be fitted with a periscope – a simple plexiglass dome was provided for surface vision and navigation. An orientation device consisting of a gyro-stabilised aircraft compass with automatic control for lateral movement and depth-keeping was fitted and performed well on trials. The master magnetic compass was fitted externally in a streamlined pod on top of the rudder assembly.

By the end of April 1945 *Schwertal* was ready for trials. All the systems worked in tests ashore and the power-plant had generated the requisite 800hp in test-bed trials. But at the end of the war the craft had to be scuttled at Plon to prevent her falling into British hands. She was subsequently raised by the Royal Navy and after a brief examination, was scrapped at Kiel. A subsequent design known as *Schwertal 2* was projected. It was even more streamlined than the original and was additionally fitted with a 25hp electric motor for silent creep speed. *Schwertal 2* never progressed beyond the drawing board. Despite the ingenious nature of the design, *Schwertal* would have probably been lethal to her operators. The problems of controlling a craft underwater at high speed are considerable. A moment's inattention and the craft could plunge beneath its test depth to destruction. Additionally the Walter turbine was not tested under operational conditions. Post-war British and American experience found that this method of propulsion was not at all suitable for submarine use.

A final German project was *Manta*, another high speed craft with a trimaran hull capable of 50+kts while planing on the surface, a submerged speed of 30+kts with a Walter turbine and an electric motor for very quiet submerged creep speed. The central hull contained the compartment for the two-man crew, while the two outer cylinders contained fuel tanks. The propulsion unit consisted of two *Schwertal 2* type units housed in the keels of the outer units. Additionally the side units were fitted with aircraft wheels to allow the craft to launch itself into the water. The armament was four torpedoes, or mines, carried on the wing surface between the outer hulls and the central body. *Manta* can only be described as a fascinating design. The whole story of midget submarines is packed with 'what if' scenarios, and that of a *Manta* storming through an Allied convoy at 50+kts, firing torpedoes or towing the 500kg mine is definitely one of the best. But *Manta* together with *Delphin* and *Schwertal* are little more than reflections of the desperate position facing Nazi Germany at the end of the war. German designers who had hitherto been sceptical of the value of midget submarines, took refuge in any design – however fantastic.

A photograph of a *Kaiten* on a loading trolley. The operator's position with periscope is just visible in the centre of the craft. In addition to be being launched from submarines and surface ships, the Japanese also planned to deploy *Kaiten* from shore sites against American invasion fleets. (US Navy)

Japanese *Kaiten* one-man submersible.

The Japanese *Kaiten*

Conception and design

Japanese submersibles represented a combination of their talent for engineering and their warrior spirit. As the Americans began to close in on the home islands, there was little Japan could do match America's awesome level of wartime production or her technical lead established in areas such as radar. Instead they looked back and sought inspiration from their own military traditions. Suicide in battle, which had always featured in the Japanese military tradition (and indeed, the western tradition) as a means of avoiding capture and thereby disgrace, was now specifically advocated in the hope that individual courage and valour could prevail over American quantitative and qualitative superiority. The inauguration of Special Attack Units, better known by the Japanese term of *Kamikaze* after the 'Divine Wind' which had saved Japan from invasion by the Mongols in 1281, was confirmation that the policy of suicide had official approval – although not everyone in the Japanese High Command was enamoured of the policy. The first such *Kamikaze* attacks were made by aircraft during the Philippines Campaign at the Battle of Leyte Gulf but the development of submersibles lay not far behind.

The need for such weapons was first realised in the Japanese submarine service where officers had been chafing under the restrictions placed on their *modus operandi*. This is not the place for a discussion on the employment of Japan's submarine fleet but suffice to say that there was dissatisfaction at submarines being employed on transport duties or attacking landing forces instead of being released against the long American supply lines. Suffice to quote Captain Kennosuke Toriso, a submarine commander who in the latter part of 1944 was an operations officer on the staff of the 6th Fleet, recalled how Japan's submariners viewed their position:

> . . . strenuous studies and efforts had been made in the Homeland on how to save the ever-deteriorating submarine situation. Typical among them was a human torpedo project which was originally advocated by two young submarine officers, Lieutenant Hiroshi Kuroke IJN and Sub-Lieutenant Sekio Nishina. Kuroke and Nishina, both graduates of the naval academy hated to see the deterioration of the submarine fleet and they decided to do what they could by volunteering to man a large torpedo themselves and ram an enemy ship.[17]

The upshot of this conversation was the development of the *Kaiten* ('Heaven-shaker') human torpedo. This was derived from the famous Type 93 'Long Lance' torpedo[18] which had caused such execution among Allied ships in the early stages of the war.

Table 7: *Kaiten* technical particulars

DISPLACEMENT:	8.2 tons submerged
DIMENSIONS:	14.75m x 1m x 1m
PROPULSION:	550bhp
SPEED:	30kts
ENDURANCE:	23,000m @ 30kts, 10,000m @ 30kts
ARMAMENT:	1550kg warhead, fitted with an inertia impact and two electric fuses.
CREW:	1[19]

The operator, who was often a trainee naval aviator, sat in a fully enclosed position containing a fixed periscope, gyro compass and controls. The *Kaiten* would be carried on a parent submarine or on specially converted warships, although in the end only one ship was so converted. The light cruiser *Kitakami* had already been converted to a fast transport with reduced armament (four 5in, eighteen 25mm AA, eight 24in torpedo tubes) carrying six 14m Daihatsu landing craft when she was torpedoed by the British submarine *Templar* in the Straits of Malacca on 27 January 1944. Though the ship was badly damaged she was not beyond repair and was thus subsequently rebuilt as a *Kaiten* carrier. Her torpedo tubes were removed, AA armament increased to sixty-seven 25mm and she was fitted with rails to carry eight *Kaiten* and a stern ramp to launch them from. This proposed use of the *Kaiten* shows that the Japanese had not given up on the idea of the war being decided by an engagement fought between big-gun battle-

Lieutenant Hiroshi Kuroke IJN (left) and Sub-Lieutenant Sekio Nishina IJN (right), the co-inventors of the *Kaiten*. Both men were subsequently killed in *Kaiten* operations. (US Navy)

The launch of a *Kaiten* over the stern of the cruiser *Kitakami* which had been specially adapted for *Kaiten* carrying duties. (Imperial War Museum: MH 6529)

ships. The *Kaiten* would have the task of whittling down the number of American battleships before the battle and finishing off the cripples afterwards (see the section on the Japanese *Ko-Hyoteki* midget submarine in the next chapter for a more detailed exposition of this strategy). But by 1944 such an engagement was the stuff of dreams. The thinking behind the operational employment of the *Kaiten* was extremely muddled. Some saw the weapon as being employed in that fleet action which the Japanese desired so much, another option was to view the weapon as a last-ditch means of defence while others, including many in the submarine service, saw the *Kaiten* as a substitute for professional competence. Captain Torisu remembered that:

> It seemed likely to me that a manned torpedo could be released from a submarine and carry out its attack far enough away from the submarine to allow the releasing vessel to remain undetected.[20]

Torisu had endured a punishing counter-attack by British destroyers off Ceylon in 1942 and had no wish to repeat the experience. Even so this last option represented an appalling waste of men and *materiel* when a little more imagination in the employment of

Japanese submarines might well have paid dividends. A couple of rigorous sessions in an attack teacher, if the Imperial Navy possessed such a thing, would have probably been far more useful.[21]

Sixteen submarines were converted to carry *Kaiten*. The number varied between classes and the conversion usually involved the removal of deck guns and hangar/catapult arrangements if fitted. The numbers of submarines converted and the number of *Kaiten* carried are as follows:

Table 8: Submarines converted to carry *Kaiten*

Submarine Class		No of Kaiten carried
KD3	(*I-118*)	2
KD3b	(*I-1156, 1157, 1159, 1160* only)	2
KD4	(*I-1162*)	2
KD5	(*I-1165*)	2
J3	(*I-8*)	4
B1	(*I-36*)	6
	(*I-37*)	4
B2	(*I-44*)	4
B3	(*I-56* and *I-58*)	4 (subsequently 6)
C2	(*I-47* and *I-48*)	4 (subsequently 6)
C3	(*I-53*)	4 (subsequently 6)

Submarine-launched *Kaitens* would be carried in cradles on the casing. Each craft would be connected to the 'mother' submarine by a flexible tube which would allow the operator to board at the last moment after receiving final instructions from the submarine's commanding officer. A telephone linked the operator with the control room until launch. After release the *Kaiten* ran at a depth of 6m on a course pre-set on its gyro by the parent submarine's navigator for a set period of time and then surfaced – the operator was now on his own. Operating a *Kaiten* was extremely difficult. The operator might elect to approach the target submerged on a hitting track in which case he had no idea of the situation on the surface. Moreover, the high speed of the *Kaiten* meant that the slightest mistake with the controls would have potentially fatal consequences. During trials of the weapon in Tokuyama Bay in the autumn of 1944, one *Kaiten* went out of control while diving: at 30kts it, and the operator, went straight to the bottom of the bay with no hope of recovery. On the other hand he could choose to make a dash to the target at periscope depth in which case his periscope wash would be visible and his speed would be limited to no more than 12kts. In theory the operator was supposed make his exit through the access hatch when he was sure that the *Kaiten* was going to hit the target. This would imply that the operator would begin to make his exit when the craft was 100m away from impact and be clear of the craft when it was 50m away. However, no-one took this provision seriously – all *Kaiten* operators intended to remain with their craft until the end. In any case a man in the water close to the explosion of a 1550kg warhead had few chances of survival. If the operator missed the target he could go round again for another go, although steering the craft at its top speed of 40kts must have been extremely difficult.

Training of the *Kaiten* pilots was initially conducted at a secret base established at Otsujima, an island off the town of Tokuyama on Honshu and some 30 prospective *Kaiten* pilots reported there in August 1944 followed by a class consisting of 200 volunteers.

Kaiten operations

As a drowning man will clutch at a straw, so the Japanese expected great things from the suicide weapons. Yet the *Kaiten* could never have the effect their name would suggest. They were incapable of independent operations. Their relative lack of endurance and non-existent habitability for the single operator meant that they could only be used once a target had been found and identified. Furthermore the *Kaiten*'s oxygen-driven propulsion system required extensive and skilled maintenance.[22] They therefore could not be deployed to isolated bases in the same way as the *Ko-Hyoteki* could, being dependent on the support services provided by the 'mother

ship', be it cruiser or submarine. There was also the question of production. *Kaiten* were quite complicated to build, with the liquid oxygen/petrol power plant requiring special attention. It would take time before sufficient stocks of the weapon were ready for operations and there was an argument for withholding operations until sufficient stocks of the *Kaiten* were available for it to make an impact. As Captain Torisu recalled:

> My voice, however, was not strong enough to persuade other staff members to share my idea of employing manned torpedoes in raiding operations at sea. As soon as a dozen of the weapons were readied, it was decided to launch the first torpedo attack on Ulithi Atoll.[23]

Ulithi was a major US Navy anchorage and in theory offered a cornucopia of targets. Yet even if sufficient number of *Kaiten* had been available, there were never enough carriers to deploy a significant number of *Kaiten* to the operational area: only one cruiser and sixteen submarines were fitted to carry them. Making allowances for refit/repair and time spent on passage between Japan and the operational area, it becomes clear that it was impossible to deploy the weapon in any number. This dilemma facing the Japanese in their use of the *Kaiten* was perfectly expressed by an operator who took part in the first attack on Ulithi on 20 November 1944:

> Daylight observation disclosed over a hundred ships at anchor in Ulithi. Though this provides a golden opportunity for the use of our human torpedoes, there but two submarines and eight human torpedoes – a very regrettable matter.[24]

The *Kaiten* carriers were also vulnerable to American attack while on passage. It was extremely doubtful that the cruiser *Kitakami* could have got into position to launch her *Kaiten* without being detected and sunk herself. The submarine carriers were no less vulnerable, being large and unwieldy with a slow diving time.

Kaiten operations fall into three distinct phases: firstly set-piece attacks against American anchorages (November 1944-February 1945); secondly deep water operations against American assault forces and amphibious forces off Okinawa (February 1945-April 1945) and thirdly deep water operations away from the combat zone against American supply lines (April 1945-September 1945). As each phase was introduced it reflected the inability of the *Kaiten* to score any successes against the American forces.

The first two operations were directed against the American anchorages at Ulithi in November 1944 and Manus, Ulithi, Hollandia and the Kossol Strait on 11 January 1945. The results were hardly auspicious: in

Kaiten mounted on the casing of the submarine *I-370* as she puts to sea on 20 February 1945. *Kaiten* crews can be seen standing on their craft waving swords and wearing the traditional *Hachimaki* headbands. Six days later *I-370* was sunk – her *Kaiten* unused. (US Navy)

the first attack nine *Kaiten* and one parent submarine, *I-37*, were sunk in return for the loss of one American oiler, the *Mississinewa*. In the second attack nineteen *Kaiten* and the parent submarine *I-48* were sunk – with no corresponding losses on the American side. The parent submarines which had returned reported that the defences at American anchorages were very much on the *qui vive*: the commanding officer of *I-56* had found the patrols so vigilant off Manus on 11 January 1945 that he could not approach the anchorage to within launching distance for the *Kaiten* so he abandoned the operation and returned.

Following this less than auspicious start the Japanese switched *Kaiten* operations to open waters hoping that the lower concentration of American ASW forces would work in their favour. The first area of operations selected was off Iwo Jima in February 1945. Yet this new move was no more successful than the last. Three submarines carrying sixteen *Kaiten* between them were deployed from 20 February but two of the parent submarines were sunk by US aircraft. The third submarine *I-44* returned, her *Kaiten* unexpended. Every time the submarine came to the surface to charge her batteries, she was spotted and put down again by aircraft. Two submarines (*I-370* and *I-368*) and ten *Kaiten* were lost, again for no American loss in return. A second operation against Iwo Jima was called off when one submarine returned with engine problems and the second was diverted while on passage to take up position as an aircraft bea-

con. In late March a *Kaiten* operation was mounted against American amphibious forces off Okinawa. Great things were hoped from this operation but two of the four carrier submarines (*I-44* and *I-56*) were sunk by American forces and the other two returned with their *Kaiten* unused.

After this dismal run of failures the Japanese made their third and last change to the *modus operandi* of the *Kaiten*. The weapons would now be employed against American supply lines away from the combat area where it was hoped that ASW concentrations would be weaker. Two *Kaiten* carriers, *I-36* and *I-47*, were despatched on 26 April. Both found convoys on 27 April and 2 May respectively. Mechanical problems bedevilled the launch of *Kaiten* both cases but there were no successes. An operation by *I-367* was equally unsuccessful. The eighth *Kaiten* operation of the war involving the carrier submarines *I-36*, *I-361*, *I-363* and *I-165* carrying a total of eighteen *Kaiten* was no more successful. Only *I-36* managed to launch her *Kaiten* on 22 and 28 June, but to no effect. *I-36* and *I-363* returned to Japan – the other two carriers were sunk.

There was only one more *Kaiten* operation before the end of the Second World War and, perversely, this was the most successful. This was also the largest operation using *Kaiten* which had been mounted to date. This operation by the *Tamon* group involved six submarines, *I-53*, *I-47*, *I-58*, *I-363*, *I-366* and *I-367*, carrying a total of thirty-three *Kaiten*. *I-53* was the first submarine to sail on 14 July 1945 and was followed by the other boats over a three-week period. Mechanical problems caused the return of *I-47*, *I-363* and *I-367* but the remainder carried on. On 21 July 1945 the assault transport *Marathon* was damaged off Okinawa by a conventional torpedo: both *I-47* and *I-367* were in the area at the time. More concrete success came on 24 July when *I-53* (Lt Cdr S Oba IJN) attacked a convoy of eight LSTs loaded with battle-weary troops of the 96th Infantry Division who were returning to Leyte from Okinawa with the destroyer *Underhill* (Lieutenant Robert M Newcomb USN) as the escort. The convoy had been sighted by a Japanese aircraft that morning and the Americans subsequently believed that the aircraft had vectored the submarine onto the LSTs. At 3.00pm on the same day what was identified as a mine was sighted dead ahead of the convoy. While the LSTs made a 45° emergency turn to port, *Underhill* bore down on the 'mine' to destroy it. While doing so, the destroyer's sonar detected multiple underwater contacts, which must have been the launch of all six *Kaiten* by *I-53*. *Underhill* commenced to drop depth charges and was rewarded by a terrific explosion. Moments later a torpedo was sighted heading straight for *Underhill*'s port bow. The torpedo was avoided but at the same time an object, identified as a submarine, was sighted dead ahead. there was no time for avoiding action and *Underhill* ploughed straight into it with cataclysmic results. The whole forward part of the ship was blown off, as far back as the forward boiler room bulkhead. Ten officers and 102 enlisted men were killed. The after part remained afloat till the evening when it was sunk by gunfire.

Three days later *I-58* (Cdr Mochitsura Hashimoto IJN) launched a pair of *Kaiten* against a tanker and heard explosions after approximately an hour. No tanker was sunk but the destroyer *Lowry* was damaged which may have been the result of a *Kaiten* attack. As a sidenote, on 30 July 1945 *I-58* scored the Japanese submarine service's single biggest success of the war when she sank the cruiser *Indianapolis* using the conventional Type 95 torpedo. On 10 and 11 August *I-58* and *I-366* launched two and three *Kaiten* respectively but scored no hits. The final *Kaiten* attack came on 12 August when *I-58* launched two against what Hashimoto thought was a seaplane carrier. In fact his target was the LSD *Oak Hill*. The *Kaiten* scraped down the side of the LSD but did not explode and was sunk by depth charges from an escort, USS *Thomas F Nickel*. In turn the *Nickel* was missed by a second *Kaiten* which passed down her port side and exploded when some distance away. Hashimoto heard the two explosions and claimed the 'seaplane carrier' as sunk. Hashimoto and the crew of *I-58* were elated by their success, but their elation turned sour on 15 August when a message in cipher was decoded announcing that Japan had surrendered.

The *Kaiten* never fulfilled the hopes of their creators. The 'exchange rate' for these operations was not auspicious: in return for the sinking of the oiler *Mississinewa* (sunk on the first *Kaiten* operation on 20th November 1944) and the destroyer *Underhill* which was sunk on the last, on 24th July 1945, the Japanese lost 8 carrier submarines and 900 officers and men. An American commentator wrote what is most apt epitaph for the *Kaiten* programme:

> . . . the Imperial Navy did a lot better with torpedoes *before* the human guidance system was added.[25]

Kairyu, *Koryu* and other weapons

Even at the end of hostilities the Japanese Navy was working on new designs of midget submarines. These were suicide weapons, conceived in the vain hope that self-sacrifice could turn back the Allied forces ranged against Japan. As such these weapons joined the band of other Japanese last-ditch weapons, such as frogmen armed with explosive charges and schoolchildren armed with bamboo pikes. The *Koryu* (Scaly Dragon) was a development of the *Ko-Hyoteki* and was armed with two 18in torpedoes.

Table 9: *Koryu* technical particulars

DISPLACEMENT:	58.4 tons (submerged)
DIMENSIONS:	26.25m x 2.04m
PROPULSION:	One shaft with contra-rotating propellers, one 150bhp diesel, one 500hp electric motor
SPEED:	8 knots (surfaced), 16 knots (submerged
ENDURANCE:	1000nm @ 8 kts, 320nm @ 16kts
ARMAMENT:	Two 457mm torpedoes
CREW:	Five

The shortage of torpedoes meant that most *Koryu* were fitted with a single explosive charge. Of the 540 ordered, only 115 were completed when the war ended: most were found in a vast graving dock at Kure which had once held the Japanese Navy's battleships

A Japanese two-man *Kairyu* abandoned after the Second World War. The only purpose-built Japanese suicide submersible, none were ever used in action. (US Navy)

A graving dock at Kure packed with the Type D *Ko-Hyoteki* better known as the *Koryu* (Scaly Dragon). The Japanese hoped that the sheer weight of numbers of these craft would overcome the immense American invasion forces. (US Navy)

in better days. None were operational and all were broken up after the war.

The *Kairyu* (Sea Dragon) was a two-man suicide craft again armed with an explosive warhead on account of the shortage of torpedoes.

Table 10: *Kairyu* technical particulars

DISPLACEMENT:	18.94/18.97 tons
DIMENSIONS:	17.28m x 1.3m
PROPULSION:	One 85bhp diesel, one 80hp electric motor
SPEED:	7.5kts (surfaced), 10kts (submerged)
RANGE:	450nm @ 10 kts, 36nm at 3kts
ARMAMENT:	Two 457mm torpedoes or one 600kg explosive charge
CREW:	Two

It was planned to have 760 *Kairyu* ready for operations by September 1945 but only 212 had been completed by the end of August 1945. As with the *Koryu* all were broken up after the end of the war.

Japanese submersibles never justified the high hopes of their proponents. Even allowing for the meagre state of Japanese official records, it easy to see why. The weapons were poorly conceived, hurriedly built and their operators inadequately trained. The underlying premise behind all the Japanese submersibles was that somehow martial valour and sheer force of character could succeed against overwhelming materiel and technological superiority. The Japanese had an almost romantic notion of the *Kaiten* roaring into battle very much as the sword-wielding *Samurai* warriors had done in Medieval times. It was not to be.

Midget Submarines

IN THE early days of submarine development, all submarines were 'midget'. But by 1914 submarines had developed sufficiently to be capable of undertaking ocean patrols of a significant length as well as long voyages – in 1910, British 'C' class submarines made the unprecedented voyage from Gosport to Hong Kong. The British *Holland 1* built in 1901 had a displacement of 113/122 tons and an armament of one 18in torpedo tube. By 1914 the 'E' class displaced 695/766 tons and were armed with four 18in torpedo tubes. The submarine had matured.

To differentiate them from submersibles reviewed in the earlier section, midget submarines possess a degree of autonomy which allows them to undertake independent operations over a period of time without the immediate support of a carrier ship or submarine.

They therefore possess the requisite navigation systems to remain at sea for prolonged periods.

The Italian *Forzatori di Basi*

Once again it was the Italians who took the lead in developing submarines for underwater assault operations. The stalemate in the Adriatic already referred to was the prime motivating factor: how to get at the four Austrian dreadnoughts without risking a fleet engagement? The *Regia Marina* possessed eleven small submarines, *Alfa*, *Beta* and the nine boats of the 'A' and 'B' classes. These boats were employed on coastal defence patrols around harbours on Italy's Adriatic coastline[1] where the threat of attack by Austrian surface vessels was considered serious.

An Italian 'B' class submarine at Venice in 1918. Built for coastal defence, these small submarines were subsequently adapted for offensive operations to break the stalemate in the Adriatic. (Museo Storico Navale, Venice)

A very rare photograph of an Italian 'B' class submarine, possibly *B 3*, in a dry dock in Venice, showing the submarine fitted with 'caterpillar tracks' for climbing over net obstacles. (A Curami)

Table 11: Italian 'B' class technical particulars

DISPLACEMENT:	60/60 tons
DIMENSIONS:	15.1m x 2.3m x 2.5m
PROPULSION:	One shaft, one 85bhp Italia petrol motor plus one 40-60hp Savigliano electric motor
SPEED:	6.9kts (surfaced), 5kts (submerged)
ENDURANCE:	128nm @ 6.9kts (surfaced), 9nm @ 5kts (submerged)
ARMAMENT:	Two 17.7in torpedo tubes. Two torpedoes carried.
CREW:	One officer and four ratings

The boats of the 'B' class were designed to be moved around the coastline by rail to where they were needed. They proved less than successful in service and were swiftly relegated to harbour duties, but one of them was brought out of 'retirement' for conversion to what must be the first assault submarine.

The *Regia Marina* had already developed the *Grillo* 'climbing boat' – a fast torpedo boat fitted with caterpillar tracks to enable it to 'climb' over net and boom defences. The idea was ingenious but suffered from one fatal flaw: the craft were exposed to detection and fire from shore batteries during their run-in. A logical progression from this idea was to fit a small submarine with the same tracks. The submarine could then approach the boom almost undetected, only to come to the surface to struggle over the net and then submerge again – hopefully undetected.

The photograph of one of the 'B' class boats above, possibly *B.3*, shows it in dry dock fitted with such caterpillar tracks. A support structure is fitted to the port and starboard side of the submarine on which is fitted a chain drive powered by the electric motor. The chain is fitted with spikes which engage with the top of the net and pull the submarine over. The submarine would approach the net at a steep bow-up angle so that the chain would engage with the net. As the chain drive engaged then the crew would flood the ballast tanks so that the weight of the submarine would pull the net down below the surface as the chain drive dragged the submarine over. In this way the disturbance on the surface would be reduced to a minimum. Once clear of the net the submarine would dive deep and then proceed into the harbour, execute the operation and then retire by the same means.

Presumably the craft was designed for an ambitious assault on Pola harbour which also involved the modification of the submarine *Argo* to carry assault frogmen and the conversion of the old battleship *Re Umberto* for use as an attack transport. The operation was cancelled when Austria sued for peace. In any case the *Mignatta* proved far more effective. However, the concept confirms the Italians' interest in this form of warfare, an interest they were to exploit to the full in the next World War.

The Italian CA and CB classes

Construction and design

In addition to the craft operated by *Decima Mas*, the *Regia Marina* had two other types of midget submarines which were employed in more conventional

Page opposite: A 'B' class submarine using its caterpillar tracks to clamber over anti-submarine netting.

operations. These were the CA/CB type submarines which were constructed as a commercial venture by the firm of Caproni but which aroused sufficient interest in the *Regia Marina* for orders to be placed. Four of the CA type and twenty-two of the CB type were constructed between 1938 and 1943 although seventy-two of the CB types had been ordered. The four CA class boats were built in two groups, *CA.1-2* and *CA.3-4*.

Table 12: CA/CB type technical particulars

	CA.1-2	*CA.3-4*	*CB Type*
DISPLACEMENT:	13.3/16.1 tons	12.6/13.8 tons	35.4/44/3 tons
DIMENSIONS:			
LENGTH:	10m	10.47	14.99
BEAM:	1.96m	1.9m	3m
DRAUGHT:	1.6m	1.83m	2.05m
ARMAMENT:	Two 450mm torpedoes	8 x 100kg charges	Two 450mm torpedoes
CREW:	2	3	4

CA.1 and *2* were fitted with a one-shaft 60bhp MAN diesel and a 25hp Marelli electric motor. They had a surface speed of 6.25kts and a top submerged speed of 5kts. *CA.3* and *4* had only the Marelli electric motor.

The role of these craft was harbour defence and patrolling in coastal waters. The CA class were highly secret and were not entered onto the Italian navy's order of battle. As far as is known, none saw any active service. However, great things were planned for *CA.2*. She was modified to be carried by the submarine *Leonardo da Vinci* and used in an attack on New York in the winter of 1943, an operation which is described later and which was frustrated by the Italian armistice. For this operation she was extensively modified, so that her particulars were as follows:

Table 13: Italian *CA.2* as modified

DISPLACEMENT:	12/14 tons
DIMENSIONS:	10m (oa) x 1.96m x 1.60m
PROPULSION:	One Marelli electric motor, 21 KW.
SPEED:	7kts (surfaced), 6kts (submerged)
ARMAMENT:	Eight 100kg explosive charges
CREW:	3

At the time of the Italian armistice in September 1943, *CA.1*, *3* and *4* were at La Spezia and *CA.2* was at Bordeaux. All were scuttled although *CA.2* was raised in 1949 and broken up.

The CB class were a good deal heavier and somewhat longer. The twenty-two CB boats reverted to diesel/electric propulsion. They were fitted with a one shaft 80bhp Isotta Fraschini diesel plus one 50bhp Brown-Boveri electric motor, and had a sur-

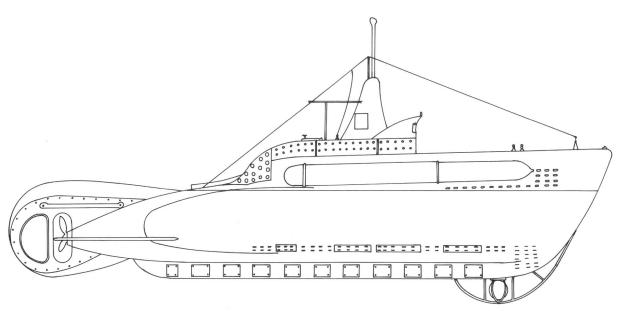

Italian CB class midget submarine.

face speed of 7.5kts and top submerged speed of 7kts. Externally they differed considerably from the four CA boats in that they were fitted with a fairing on top of the pressure hull together with a small conning tower. This allowed members of the crew to stand safely on the hull while manoeuvring on the surface. The armament of two 450mm torpedoes were carried in external cages on top of the craft, flush with the casing. This arrangement, extremely practical, meant that the craft did not have to be removed from the water for the weapons to be fitted.

The CB class were constructed in two groups. Boats 1 to 6 were all built in Milan by Caproni and delivered to the *Regia Marina* between January and May 1941. There then followed a two-year halt in the programme until the next boat, *CB.7*, was delivered on 1 August 1943. The remaining fourteen units were delivered throughout 1943. Undoubtedly the threat of invasion following the collapse of Axis forces in North Africa stimulated the revival of interest in the programme.

CB boat operations

The wartime service of the CB class was varied. Boats *CB.1, 2, 3, 4, 5* and *6* were transported by road and rail to the Romanian port of Costanza on the Black Sea where they arrived on 2 May 1942. Operating from Costanza they supported the right flank of the

Lower left: CB.3 about to be returned to the water after refit at Costanza in the summer of 1942. (Dott. Achille Rastelli)

Lower right: A CB being hoisted out of the water at Costanza. This photograph shows the protective guard fitted around the hydrophone under the bow. (Dott. Achille Rastelli)

The same *CB* but photographed from the starboard quarter. This photograph shows the single propeller, rudder and control surfaces. (Dott. Achille Rastelli)

A view of the starboard quarter of *CB.1* showing the starboard torpedo tube 'broken' for maintenance or loading. The after section of the tube contained the compressed air firing equipment. (Dott. Achille Rastelli)

German Army and enforced a naval blockade of Sevastopol throughout the summer of 1942. On 15 June 1942 *CB.3* (TV Giovanni Sorrentino) attacked a Soviet submarine without success but three days later STV Attilio Russo in *CB.2* attacked and sank the Soviet submarine *SC-208*. On 25 August 1934 *CB.4* commanded by TV Armando Sibille attacked and sank the Soviet submarine *SC-207* south of Tarahankut. On the debit side *CB.5* was sunk in an air raid on 13 June 1942 when she was torpedoed at Yalta by Soviet aircraft.

The five survivors of the Black Sea boats were handed over to Romania in September 1943 only to be taken over by the Soviets on 30 August 1944 when Romania surrendered. The boats are reported to have remained in Soviet service until 1955. Of the remaining boats, *CB.8*, *9*, *10*, *11* and *12* were all surrendered intact to the British at Taranto in September 1943. *CB.7* was at Pola where she was captured by the Germans, transferred to the Italian Social Republic (Mussolini's German-backed regime in northern Italy) and then cannibalised for spare parts in order to complete *CB.13*. *CB.13*, *14*, *15* and *17* were all destroyed in air raids in 1945. *CB.16* was transferred to the Italian Social Republic and put into service. On 1 October 1944 she grounded near Sennigallia on the Adriatic coast where she was captured by British forces. *CB.18* and *19* were broken up post-war in Venice; *CB.30* was captured by Yugoslav partisans at Pola and her subsequent fate is unknown. *CB.21* was rammed and sunk by a German *MFP* (motorised transport ferry) while *en route* to Ancona to surrender to the Allies. Lastly *CB.22* was captured at Trieste at the end of the war, for many years her hull lay derelict on a quayside until 1950 when she was transferred to the Trieste War Museum where she is on display today.

The CA/CB types were an entirely workable design. They proved themselves quite effective during operations in the Black Sea and, had they been available in any numbers at the time of the invasion of Italy, they might have acquitted themselves well and disrupted the landings.

CA.2 and the attack on New York

The armistice which the Italian government concluded with the Allies in September 1943 ended plans for the employment of a CA-type submarine in a most daring operation. The CA/CB boats were operated by the regular submarine arm of the *Regia Marina*, but it

A view of the high conning tower of a *CB* boat at Costanza. The rating is making adjustments to the boat's wireless aerial. The access hatch on the top of the conning tower was primarily intended for observation when the boat was running on the surface. Access to the boat was usually gained via a larger hatch forward of the conning tower. (Dott. Achille Rastelli)

An Italian *CB* class midget submarine, *CB.6*, out of the water for repair at Costanza on the Black Sea in April 1942. In this picture part of the conning tower has been removed for maintenance. The open gratings at the port side are the free flooding holes to the port ballast tanks. Note the very boat-like shape of the hull. (Dott. Achille Rastelli)

Above: A group of *CB*s at Costanza in the summer of 1942. The craft in the background appears to have a fairing around her forward hatch to prevent water pouring down into the boat. (Dott. Achille Rastelli)

Upper right: The squadron insignia of the Italian Black Sea *CB* flotilla. When the Germans and their Italian allies were forced to retreat in the Autumn of 1942 the craft were abandoned and subsequently taken over by the Russians. (Dott. Achille Rastelli)

Right: A CB type submarine under way along the Crimean coast in the summer of 1942. The Black Sea was to prove the most fruitful area of operations for the CB craft. (Dott. Achille Rastelli)

The Italian midget submarine *CA 2* as modified for carriage on the *Leonardo da Vinci* for the planned attack on New York.

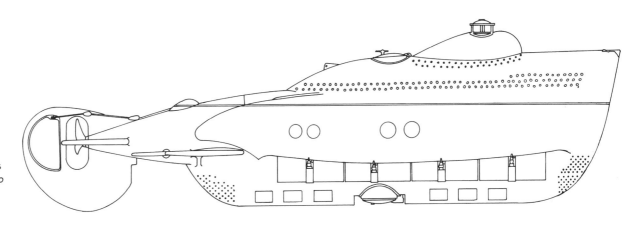

The Italian *CA.2* lashed down on the forecastle of *Leonardo da Vinci* at Bordeaux in the spring of 1943 during preparations for the attack on New York. (Dott. Achille Rastelli)

A view of the well built into *Leonardo da Vinci*'s casing to house the *CA.2*. The 'bandstand' railings allowed (relatively) safe access to the craft for maintenance purposes while on passage. (Dott. Achille Rastelli)

was inevitable that sooner or later *Decima Mas* planners would take an interest in the employment of these craft–even though they were not designed for special operations. Their plan was extravagant, even by the standards of an organisation specialising in the audacious. By the summer of 1942 harbour defences in the Mediterranean were at such a high state that it would be almost suicidal to use a craft which had not been operationally proven. Accordingly the planners at the Bocche di Serchio cast their eyes further afield to where the eastern seaboard of the United States beckoned. Not since the Anglo-American war of 1812 had an attack been planned against the mainland USA. Not only did this area offer an abundance of targets, but it had not experienced an attack by underwater assault units. Consequently defences (in the United States port defence was the responsibility of the US Army) were not a patch on anything encountered in the Mediterranean. A successful attack on an American port (New York was the favourite) would have immense political and psychological consequences and force the Americans to devote considerable resources to harbour defence. Borghese decided on the employment of one CA class submarine and a number of *Gamma* assault frogmen. The *CA.2* and the frogmen would be released some way outside the harbour, the frogmen being given a 'tow' by the submarine and in turn helping the *CA.2* through any nets and into the Hudson River after which they would attack such targets as presented themselves.

But how to convey the tiny *CA.2* across the Atlantic? The obvious solution was to carry the craft on the deck of another larger submarine. The *Leonardo da Vinci* was chosen and had a well constructed on her casing forward of the conning tower in which the CA craft settled snugly, being held down by retaining clamps which could be operated from inside the submarine. At this stage the Italians asked if the Germans would like to contribute a U-boat so that two CAs could be employed. After due consideration Donitz refused, but he did offer the Italians full co-operation in providing up-to-date intelligence on defences on America's east coast. In July 1942 *Leonardo da Vinci* (TV Gianfranco Prioroggia) successfully made the passage through the Straits of Gibraltar and arrived at Bordeaux where *CA.2* had been sent by rail. The modifications to her hull were carried out at Bordeaux under the supervision of *Maggiore del Genio Navale* Fenu before she was ready for trials in September. The trials took place at La Pallice and Verdon and were a complete success. It was found to be quite safe to release the CA when the *Da Vinci* was at a depth of 12m. The smaller craft, being positively buoyant, simply rose to the surface, where she was boarded by her crew who transferred over in a rubber dinghy. To recover the CA the *Da Vinci* positioned herself underneath the midget,

observations being taken through the periscope, and slowly surfaced. It was a manoeuvre requiring some dexterity and skill and was personally supervised by none other than Borghese who had assumed command of the submarine for the trials. While further training was taking place and adjustments were being made to *CA.2*, *Leonardo da Vinci* was lost on 25 May 1943 in a depth charge attack by the British destroyer HMS *Active* and the frigate *Ness*. There was no time to convert another submarine for the role before the armistice brought all operations to a halt. Of all the 'what ifs' of the Second World War, this operation that never took place is one of the greatest.

The Japanese *Ko-Hyoteki*

Genesis of the design

The Japanese midget submarines, *Ko-Hyoteki*, were in a class of their own in terms of development. However, in operations they were not particularly successful and as the course of the war turned against Japan, they were withdrawn from offensive operations and employed on harbour and local defence. This role was contrary to their purpose, midget submarines being offensive weapons of surprise, and they incurred considerable losses to American air and naval patrols. It was a sad end for a force which had promised much and which had not been used to its fullest potential.

The development of a midget submarine was the idea of Captain Yokoo Takeyoshi IJN. Yokoo drew upon his experience of the Russo-Japanese War and considered that piloted torpedoes would be a considerable value in sinking ships inside a defended anchorage. His idea was seized upon by Captain Kishemoto Kanji who was in charge of the Second Section of the First Main Division of the Navy Technical Department (responsible for torpedo development) who turned a theoretical proposition into reality.

Kishemoto put his proposal to Commander Asama Toshihide, a specialist in torpedo development, and ordered construction to begin in great secrecy. In brief Kishemto's proposal was for a 'mother' torpedo which would close with the enemy battlefleet and attack at high speed and at short range. After consideration it followed that the weapon had to have the following basic characteristics: firstly, to be effective it had to have a speed 1.5 times that of the main speed of the American battlefleet–therefore it had to have a speed of 30kts submerged; secondly, it had to be armed with two torpedo tubes; thirdly, the weapon's range was dictated by the distance between the gun ranges of the two fleets (in other words outside the range of the IJN battlefleet's main armament) and was therefore set at 35nm; and fourthly the craft had to have sufficient habitability to remain in the area of operations to be recovered afterwards.

A *Ko-Hyoteki* raised by the Americans from inside Pearl Harbor. The photographs shows the 'washboard' effect on the hull of depth charging as well as damage, forward, inflicted by ramming. This *Ko-Hyoteki* ended up being buried as part of a breakwater. (US Navy)

The upshot of this brief was the production of a research vehicle which was expected to achieve the required speed of 30kts using small, light, high-capacity batteries and an electric motor of similar characteristics. Tests using this unmanned vehicle were successful and in the summer of 1932, Kishemoto had the opportunity to present his plan to the Chief of the Navy General Staff, Admiral Fushimi-no-miya-Hiroyasu, brother of Emperor Hirohito. Approaching the professional head of the Navy directly was most unusual, but Kishemoto felt compelled to do so in order to maintain secrecy around the project and to gain sufficient backing in order to drive the project through the Navy's bureaucracy.

Fushimi gave his approval, after noting that the crew had to be provided with a means of escape. At this stage it would be well to note that, unlike the *Kaiten* and her derivatives, these weapons were not dedicated suicide weapons, in Japanese parlance *Tokko Heiki* ('Special Attack Weapons'). Suicide was an integral part of the Japanese military code, but was to be resorted to only cases of supreme urgency to avoid the disgrace of failure or the dishonour of capture. It was only when defeat was staring the Japanese government in the face in the summer of 1944, that suicide weapons were adopted as a means of halting the American advance.

Fushimi's approval meant that design of a prototype could begin. Vice-Admiral Sugi, head of the Navy Technical Department, was ordered to assemble a committee which was to meet in conditions of extreme secrecy with Kishemoto as the chairman. The four members of the committee were: Commander Katayama Arika, responsible for hull development,

Commander Asama Toshihide for torpedo development, and Commander Nawa Takeshi and Commander Yamada Kiyoshi for propulsion development. It is interesting to note that all these officers subsequently attained flag rank.

The design team were soon confronted with a number of difficulties for which they had no existing body of experience to draw on. How could the deadly battery exhaust gasses be vented? How could the steering mechanism be simplified? How could submerged trim be maintained? These were just some of the problems the team had to solve. Nevertheless, in what was the amazingly short time of two months the team had worked out the parameters for the prototype: a battery-driven torpedo-shaped craft with a top submerged speed of 25kts and a radius of action of 60km. By August 1933 the prototype, built by the Torpedo Experimental Division at Kure, was ready. Tests were carried out in the Inland Sea amid conditions of considerable secrecy. At first the trials were unmanned with the craft being controlled by an automatic depth-keeping mechanism. Performance was satisfactory, with a speed of 24.85kts being recorded.[2] This was, and still is, the highest speed ever recorded by a battery-powered midget submarine.

In October Lieutenant Commander Kato Ryonosuke and Engineer Sub-Lieutenant Harada Shin became the first naval personnel to operate the craft. These trials continued throughout the winter of 1933 and into the summer of 1934 and proved that the craft had considerable potential. However, there were some problems which needed to be sorted out: the periscope depth had to be increased since the craft tended to broach when in this condition, the depth-keeping machinery was unreliable and both operators felt that an increase in range was desirable. The first problem was overcome by constructing a conning tower on the torpedo-shaped hull and by lengthening the periscope. However, this also had the side effect of increasing resistance and taking 2kts off the top submerged speed. Improvements were made to the depth-keeping machinery but the cruising radius remained the same. The trials were finished in December 1934. The prototype was taken ashore and stored in a sealed warehouse at the Torpedo Experimental Division at Kure. All documents and plans relating to the project were likewise stored in

The interior of a *Ko-Hyoteki* captured by the Australians at Sydney in June 1942. The view shows the control room looking forward with the periscope and periscope well in the centre. (Australian War Memorial)

sealed safes. The Navy had decided to re-test the performance of the craft by building a second series and then comparing the results.

At the same time the Navy was refining the tactical doctrine under which the boats would be employed. The original concept of the craft delivering massed torpedo attacks from short range was declared valid but the problem remained of how the craft were to be transported to the operational area. The solution lay in the construction of ships specially configured to carry the midgets, which would accompany the battle-fleet but would deploy at the appropriate time. Three such ships were ordered under the Second Fleet Replenishment Plan of 1934, and a fourth was added in the Third Replenishment Programme of 1937 but her construction was altered and she was completed as a seaplane tender. The three original ships were named *Chitose*, *Chiyoda* and *Mizuho* and were declared to be seaplane tenders which excluded them from the limitations set down in the Washington Naval Treaty. The fourth ship was named *Nisshin*. Each ship could function in the role of seaplane tender but a quick conversion programme would enable each to carry twelve of the midget submarines. As each submarine carried two torpedoes, totalling ninety-six torpedoes in all, this should have been enough to do enough damage so as to whittle down the American superiority.

Meanwhile, the trials continued under conditions of extreme secrecy. The Admiral Superintendent at the Kure Naval Yard was given nothing but the merest details of the craft despite the fact that all the tests were carried out at the Torpedo Experimental Division, an organisation of which he was nominally in charge. Only selected personnel could enter the building and those authorised to do so were issued with passes containing their photograph and finger-prints. Documents concerning the project were never sent by post, only by reliable courier. No officer with a rank lower than that of Commander participated in the trials which took place in the Inland Sea, so great was the desire to ensure secrecy.

At times the secrecy almost gave the game away. The craft had to be called something, so a number of cover names were introduced such as *TB Mokei* ('TB' Model), *Tokushu Hyoteki* (Special Target), *A Hyoteki* ('A' Target) and *Taisen Bakugeki Hyoteki* (Anti-Submarine Bombing Target). This last name nearly had disasterous consequences:

> Unfortunately the designation came to the notice of the staff of the First Air Fleet who saw in it a perfect vehicle for their aircrew to practice attacks on sub-marines. Accordingly a demand for the craft made it's way through the Navy's bureaucracy and it was only after some difficulty that the aviators were persuaded to withdraw their request.[3]

The result of the first and second series of tests on the two prototypes was that the Navy General Staff adopted a five-point programme for future development:

(1) On the basis of the prototype trials, two more test boats were to be constructed at Kure to conduct trials under as near operational conditions as could be replicated.

(2) If these trials were successful, then the crews should work up the methods used to launch the craft from the carriers.

(3) All being well, forty-eight such craft should then be constructed as quickly as possible.

(4) Facilities for the storage and maintenance of the craft were to be constructed at Kure, secrecy being of paramount importance.

(5) Selection and training of personnel should begin at once to provide a pool of trained operators.

But it was to be nearly four years before any further significant developments took place in the programme. By then Japan's position in the international community had altered dramatically. Japan had resigned from the League of Nations in 1932, had given notice of their intention to abandon the system of naval limitation by treaty and was continuing its campaign of conquest in China – to considerable but ineffective international disapproval. Simultaneously the IJN was engaged in an urgent and radical reconstruction programme following the loss of the destroyer *Tomozuru*,[4] the 'Fourth Fleet Incident' in September 1935 and the failure of the medium-pressure turbine blades in the destroyer *Asashio* in December 1937. There was therefore not much in the way of time or resources for midget submarine construction.

It was not until the summer of 1939 that the Navy Minister ordered the two experimental boats from the Navy Yard at Kure. The first was launched in April 1940 and the second at the end of June. Trials begun at once in the Inland Sea with Lieutenant Sekido Yoshimitsu and Engineer Lieutenant Hori Toshio forming the crew. Following trials in the Inland Sea, the next stage was the launching trials from *Chiyoda* which had completed in December 1938. While the two experimental craft were nearing completion, *Chiyoda*'s stern was modified, very like that of a whaling factory ship, to form a launching ramp. The craft would be rolled down this ramp, stern first, into the water. First trials at Iyo-Nada in Hiroshima Bay proved satisfactory, and from July to the end of August 1940 attack trials were carried out in the rougher waters of the Bungo Strait. Initially an unmanned craft was launched off *Chiyoda*'s stern more than ten times before Sekido and Hori undertook the first manned launch. The trials were a complete success. *Chiyoda* launched the craft in various sea states

and while steaming at speeds of between 12 and 20kts. In all cases a comparatively flat angle of entry into the water was measured and the craft emerged about 1000m astern of the 'mother' craft and was seen to move away under its own power. However, Sekido was critical of certain aspects of the craft's performance. Many of the instruments did not appreciate the rough nature of the launch and he noted that at periscope depth in a running sea, pitching and rolling was very evident, making target acquisition very difficult. The craft also showed a regrettable tendency to broach at the most inappropriate moment:

> . . . the conning tower was always exposed which cannot in fact be called submerging . . . for me the impression did not disappear for a long time that an attack on the ocean was very, very difficult.[5]

Nevertheless, the observers, including Vice-Admiral Toyoda Soemu (Chief of the Navy Technical Department) were favourably impressed. Toyoda had hitherto been an unreserved sceptic of the whole project but after seeing the trials from *Chiyoda* revised his opinion considerably.

One feature of the Japanese programme was constant modification and the period after the *Chiyoda* trials was no exception. Improvements were carried out to the hydroplane motors to improve submerged control and the instruments were made more robust, together with a host of other modifications. But at this stage there was a certain degree of conflict between the technicians and the operators. The technicians pressed for further improvements and modifications which would have required an increase in size and displacement, while the operators argued that any increase in size would have considerable knock-on effects on the 'mother ships', on storage, launching and a host of other areas. Moreover the, world situation did not permit the trials period to be extended for purely 'academic reasons'. This was a weapon and was required for sea.

The operators won. On 15 November 1940 the craft were formally adopted by the Navy and given the name *Ko-Hyoteki*. Things now moved apace. On 10 October 1940 a further ten boats were ordered, *Nos. 3 to 12*, and in December *Nos. 13 to 26* were ordered. Enough *Ko-Hyoteki* were now on order for three carriers to be converted and armed. At the same time training for the officers and men began directed by Commander Kato Ryanosuke under the overall command of Captain Harada Kaku, commanding officer of the *Chiyoda*.

The first group of thirteen officers and petty officers reported to *Chiyoda* in November 1940 and practical sea training began in January 1941, the intervening time being occupied with classroom instruction. By March 1941 their training was complete and the second group of twenty-two officers and petty officers, together with twelve technicians, arrived in April. At the same time the instruction was moved to Karasukojima near Kure. Theoretical instruction was given at the Torpedo Experimental Division of Kure Navy Yard while instruction in tactics and deployment was given at the submarine school. Basic sea training aboard the tug *Kure Maru* then followed before the operators moved to the real thing, operating from *Chiyoda* or *Nisshin*, now working in her original role. The second group's training was completed in August. By this stage the programme was suddenly accelerated owing to the deterioration in relations with the United States and three more *Ko-Hyoteki*, configured solely for training purposes, were ordered to meet the acceleration in the programme.

Construction and design

But what were these craft, on which the Japanese had expended so much effort and kept so secret? Externally the craft resembled a torpedo with tapered ends surmounted by a conning tower amidships. Apart from the conning tower there was no superstructure of any kind. To reduce water resistance the only fittings on the hull were a number of cleats cut from 12mm steel and welded to the hull. Fore and aft the torpedo tubes and propellers were fitted with shields to protect them while a 9.5m ballast keel was welded to the underside of the hull.

The *Ko-Hyoteki* was a single-hull midget submarine. The pressure hull was all-welded, of 8mm cold rolled steel plates of MS44 quality. Weight reduction was extremely important in all stages of the craft's construction and Commander Katayma Ariki proved himself resourceful and ingenious in achieving this without compromising the operational effectiveness of the craft or safety standards. All-welded construction was one way Katayama saved weight. Another was the use of 2.6mm steel in non pressure-bearing parts of the structure instead of 8mm steel. The internal bulkheads which divided the *Ko-Hyoteki* into several compartments were gas-tight but not watertight since the panels between the stiffeners were only

1.2mm thick. The *Ko-Hyoteki* was built to very fine tolerances and despite the necessity to reduce weight, the collapse depth was still calculated as 200m and the safe diving depth as 100m. These parameters gave a safety coefficient 1.4 times greater than that of other Japanese submarines.

Compared to the trials version, the length was increased by 6cm and the interior diameter in the control room section by 2.6cm. Increased hydrodynamic performance was obtained by drawing in the sides of the bow to produce an oval as opposed to a circular shape. The fore and after ends of the pressure hull were closed by convex bulkheads, beyond which was one external compartment, bow and stern. At the bow this compartment was used for the main ballast tank and the reserve ballast tank but the compartment at the stern was a free-flooding space.

The hull was divided into three sections in order to facilitate construction and fitting out. The forward section contained the *Ko-Hyoteki*'s *raison d'etre*, two 45.7cm torpedo tubes mounted one above the other. The prototypes had been fitted with 53.3cm tubes for the Type 89 torpedo but the introduction into service of the 45.7cm Type 97 oxygen-driven torpedo seemed another golden opportunity for saving weight and so it was adopted. The torpedo tubes were 5.4m long, roughly the length of the compartment, and were of a most unusual design. Unlike conventional torpedo tubes which are fitted with bow and stern caps, the tubes in the *Ko-Hyoteki* were simply a tube with a spherical casting riveted to the rear end in place of the breech which contained a tail stop with a thick rubber baffle and a fitting for the air impulse check valve. There was no bow cap: the torpedoes were simply slid into place tail first. The simplicity of the design meant that the tubes were free-flooding so there was no need for complicated flooding and venting arrangements – another weight saving – while the warhead of the torpedo projected about 30mm from the forward end of the tube, thus providing a streamlined finish.

The torpedoes' gyro angle and depth setting was adjusted from within the control room by means of mechanical linkages and shafts connected to the gyro

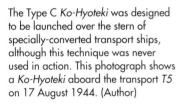

The Type C *Ko-Hyoteki* was designed to be launched over the stern of specially-converted transport ships, although this technique was never used in action. This photograph shows a *Ko-Hyoteki* aboard the transport *T5* on 17 August 1944. (Author)

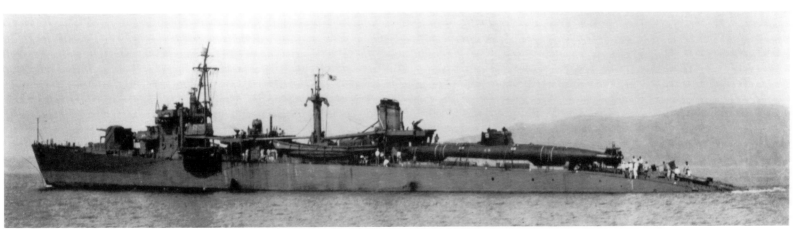

and depth-keeping spindles in the torpedo tubes while indicators in the control room monitored the adjusted angles. The torpedoes were fired by air pressure, each tube having a firing tank containing 69.4 litres of air. There was only one problem with the firing arrangements and one which was the subject of bitter complaint by the crews: since there were no arrangements to vent the tubes internally, a stream of bubbles appeared on the surface each time a torpedo was fired. Hardly ideal for a craft engaged in covert operations but a inevitable result of the need to save weight in the design.

The *Ko-Hyoteki*'s main ballast tank formed the space around the two torpedo tubes. This contained 1336 litres of water and was usually filled in the depot ship before launch because the small size of the inlet valve made it very difficult to flood the tank while at sea. When the main ballast tank was blown the bow of the *Ko-Hyoteki* came up very quickly while the stern remained unmoved–unsurprising given that the stern had no ballasting arrangements and contained the weight of the motor. Due to this extreme bow-up angle, it was usually some time before the conning tower broke surface. To deal with this problem a 416-litre emergency tank was fitted under the control room.

Behind the compartment containing the torpedo tubes and their associated firing tanks was the compartment containing the reserve ballast tank, which automatically filled when the torpedoes were fired to compensate for the loss of weight. However, the size of the inlet valve was insufficient to permit quick filling and it was all too often the case that a *Ko-Hyoteki* would bob to the surface after firing. Crews tried increasing speed on firing but the *Ko-Hyoteki* persisted in broaching: another source of complaint.

The centre section of the boat was divided into three separate compartments: the forward battery room, the control room and conning tower and the after battery room. Unlike many types of midget submarine in other navies, the *Ko-Hyoteki* used electric power for both submerged and surface propulsion. The main battery was thus the boat's sole source of power. It consisted of 192 trays, each cell consisting of two 2v cells. The cells were connected in parallel-series combinations: 136 trays (75 per cent of the battery) were installed in the after battery compartment and the remaining 56 trays in the forward compartment. The trays were arranged along the sides of the craft to facilitate inspection and maintenance while under way. Battery ventilation was provided by suctioning the air from the forward battery compartment, forcing it through a cell containing a hydrogen absorption agent and then discharging it into the after battery compartment after cooling and mixing with HP air. This was not the most ideal hydrogen absorption system but it was considered acceptable since the

boat would only have to be 'at sea' for a few hours. When the battery was charged ashore or aboard the depot ship a port in the *Ko-Hyoteki*'s side provided additional ventilation.

The forward and after battery compartments also contained the trimming tanks, a 357-litre tank forward and a 257-litre tank aft. Flooding and pumping out was done via the bilge pump but this had the unfortunate side effect of clogging the system with mud. An additional pump, driven by the periscope motor, was also fitted. Trimming was difficult because the distance between the two tanks was comparatively small. To correct this 1421kg of lead was carried in the forward battery compartment on trolleys which could be shifted manually to compensate for changes in the boat's weight. There were also two balance tanks, one forward and one aft, holding 232 and 180 litres respectively. The forward tank was located under the torpedo tubes, the after one under the main motor.

The control room was located between the two battery compartments and directly beneath the conning tower containing the single access hatch. It contained all the controls for the *Ko-Hyoteki* such as the automatic and manual depth-control gear, the helm, the master gyro compass and the directional gyro indicator, the firing controls, periscope motor, trim pump, HP air manifold, small crystal radio set, hydrogen detector and periscope.

The periscope was a marvel of miniaturisation produced by the Japan Optical Manufacturing Co to a design of the Naval Technical Laboratory. The all-pervasive secrecy surrounding the project required that the device be named *Toku Megane* ('Special Glasses'). The periscope was 3.05m long and had a diameter of 92mm. It had magnifications of x 1.5 and x 6. The periscope projected out of the conning tower for about 30cm and was enclosed in a streamlined casing to reduce resistance. In addition to the periscope the *Ko-Hyoteki* were also fitted with an echo sounder (the use of which would have been a complete giveaway, so it is difficult to see why this was fitted in a craft intended for covert operations), and a primitive non-directional hydrophone. The only other concession to navigation was the fitting of a tiny chart table. Nevertheless, the periscope, hydrophone and chart table were sufficient for covert operations in confined waters. Above the control room was the pressure-tight conning tower which consisted of two vertical cylinders arranged one behind the other. The forward cylinder was the access hatch while the after cylinder contained the periscope. At the after end of the conning tower was the aerial for the UHF radio which could be raised to a height of 8m by a worm gear in the control room.

A number of *Ko-Hyoteki* were converted to training boats and were slightly modified. The size of the after

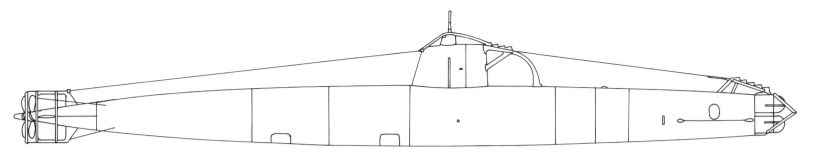

Japanese *Ko-Hyoteki* Type A midget submarine.

battery was reduced and the space saved was used to accommodate two instructor officers and a class of six or seven trainees. An additional tank was fitted to compensate for the loss of weight due to the removal of the battery. The size of the conning tower was also increased and a second periscope fitted for the use of the instructor.

The stern section was separated from the after section by an insulated bulkhead and contained the single electric motor, manufactured by the Toshiba Corporation and weighing about 1.5 tons. At 1800rpm the motor produced 600hp and was controlled from the control room by manual switches. Depending on battery combinations the motor drove the *Ko-Hyoteki* at a maximum speed of 24kts. Astern power at 5kts was also available. Reduction gears in the ratio of 5:5:1 transmitted the revolutions to the single propeller shaft. The gearbox was located aft of the motor room in the freeflooding space at the stern. At the end of the shaft were two contra-rotating propellers, the forward one turning in a left-handed cycle and the after one in a right-handed cycle. The forward screw was slightly larger than the after one, 1.35m metres as opposed to 1.25m. Vertical and horizontal stabiliser fins with rudders and hydroplanes were installed just forward of the propellers. The whole assembly was carefully thought out and designed so as not to offer any projections which could snag in a net.

The *Ko-Hyoteki* were possibly the most sophisticated and well-designed midget submarines used by any of the belligerents in the Second World War. The designers were working to a clear and precise operational requirement which they fulfilled. Naturally there were some shortcomings in the design – poor submerged control and lack of internal venting for the torpedo tubes were two such aspects. But no design ever manages to completely fulfil the requirements of its designers and its operators: conflicts were inevitable. The comparison is often made, unfavourably, with the British *X-Craft*. This comparison is unfair because *X-Craft* were designed for long-range extended operations while *Ko-Hyoteki* were designed for a short and decisive naval engagement and this is reflected in the design.

As the war progressed it became clear that there would never be an engagement between the Japanese and American fleets of the kind for which the Japanese had so assiduously planned and hoped for. It also became clear as Japan's sphere of influence widened in the Pacific area, that there could be a number of uses for the *Ko-Hyoteki* other than high-profile (and wasteful) attacks on shipping. Harbour defence was one such role which presented itself, particularly as from 1943 onwards the Americans assumed the offensive. The adoption of such a role meant substantial modifications to the craft to take account of it. It proved impossible to incorporate these modifications within the hull of the Type A *Ko-Hyoteki* so a variant known as Type B was constructed. The Type B differed in several major respects and comparative dimensions are given in Table 14.

Table 14: *Ko-Hyoteki* technical particulars

	Type A	*Type B*
DESIGN BEGUN:	1938	1942
FIRST BOAT COMPLETED:	1939	1943
LENGTH (oa):	23.9m	24.9m
BEAM (max):	1.85m	1.88m
DEPTH (CT to keel):	3.1m	3.1
DISPLACEMENT (submerged):	46 tons	50 tons
MAIN BATTERY (type/no of cells):	Special D/224	Special D/224
MAIN MOTOR (hp):	600	600
MAX SUBMERGED SPEED:	24kts	18.5kts
DIVING DEPTH:	100m	100m
ARMAMENT:	Two 45.7cm torpedo tubes	Two 45.7cm torpedo tubes
NO OF TORPEDOES:	2	2
HP AIR FLASKS (litres capacity x no):	430 x 2	430 x 2
PERISCOPE (length):	3.05m	3.05m
GENERATOR:	N/A	40hp/25kW x 1
CREW:	2	3
ENDURANCE:	Negligible	1-2 days[6]

The Type B was not much bigger but contained a third crewman who was to be an Engine Room Artificer or Chief Engine Room Artificer, a reflection of the need for proper management of all the equip-

Ko-Hyoteki abandoned in the Aleutians in June 1943. These sophisticated craft never really found a role once the Japanese Command opted for a surprise attack on the American fleet at Pearl Harbor. The photograph gives an excellent view of the arrangement of the two bow torpedo tubes- one above the other. (US Navy)

ment onboard. The addition of a third member of the crew coupled with the minimal increase in size and increase in endurance meant that conditions on board would be very cramped indeed and this must have had an effect on operational efficiency. The other significant alteration was the addition of a 40hp/25kW generator and a 0.6-ton fuel tank. This permitted the charging of the battery while at sea, although this took an unacceptable eighteen hours, and would also permit direct drive while the boat was on the surface, thus increasing endurance to 300-350 miles at 5-6kts. However, the weight of the generator meant a reduction in maximum submerged speed from 24 to 18.5kts. The Type B was a prototype which went into production as the Type C *Ko-Hyoteki*. About thirty-six of these boats were built at Ourazaki near Kure before the autumn of 1944.[7] Development did not stop there. A minelaying *Ko-Hyoteki* called *M-Kanamono* was built in 1944 and carried four Type 2 or Type 3 submarine-laid mines instead of torpedoes. Only one of these craft was constructed. Even writing with all the benefits of hindsight, the failure to proceed with this project represented a considerable lost opportunity for the Japanese. As a covert minelayer the *Ko-Hyoteki* would have been quite successful and would have caused a good deal of trouble to the Americans – the Germans made the same mistake with their *Biber* one-man submarine.

Ko-Hyoteki operations

The *Ko-Hyoteki* were never employed as their designers had envisaged. In February 1941 Grand Admiral Yamamoto Isoroku, one of the most far-sighted and innovative officers in the Imperial Japanese Navy, assumed command of the Combined Fleet. One of his first acts was to throw out the plan for a Jutland-style battlefleet engagement at sea and everything that

went with it – including the *Ko-Hyoteki*. Instead Japan would destroy the American fleet at their moorings at Pearl Harbor by means of a surprise attack using carrier-borne aircraft.

Thus at a stroke the *Ko-Hyoteki* were made redundant. However, the determination which had carried the designers and operators through the development and trials programme would not allow the project to be quietly abandoned. Sub-Lieutenant Iwasa Naoji, one of the operators, considered the possibility of employing the *Ko-Hyoteki* in attacking warships in defended anchorages. Why, he reasoned, could they not attack American ships at Pearl Harbor, Manila, San Francisco and at a host of other bases? Iwasa discussed his ideas with Commander Ryonosuke Kato, in charge of *Ko-Hyoteki* training, who passed the plan to Captain Harada. The next stage was for Iwasa to request an interview with Yamamoto and it says much for the admiral that he was prepared to devote time to hearing the earnest Sub-Lieutenant out. Despite Iwasa's eloquence and obvious enthusiasm, Yamamoto turned the plan down, not because he doubted the potential of the craft but because did not believe that the operators could be rescued.

The *Ko-Hyoteki* men were not disheartened. In September 1941 Harada moved *Chitose* to the Sea of Aki in the Inland Sea, an area which bore a superficial resemblance to Pearl Harbor. Here the *Ko-Hyoteki* were put through their paces at entering a simulated defended harbour and returning to a blacked-out *Chitose*. Although the exercises were a success, it was realised that the restricted range of the craft meant that *Chitose* could not be risked near to Pearl Harbor: the Americans would be sure to be suspicious of a lone Japanese warship operating so far from home.

The solution lay in carrying the *Ko-Hyoteki* on the casing of a 'C1' class submarine.[8] The *Ko-Hyoteki* rested, facing aft, on a cradle constructed on the casing aft of the conning tower. This was not an unusual method of carriage for a midget submarine: Italy, Britain and Germany used similar methods, and indeed it is extremely logical to use another submarine as the carrier, thus taking advantage of the submarine's inherent stealth qualities. Where the Japanese design was unique was in the design of a mating collar between the *Ko-Hyoteki* and the 'parent' submarine. An arrangement of two close-fitting cylinders enabled access between the midget and the carrier while the submarine was submerged and thus allowed maintenance to be carried out while the submarine was on passage to the target area – a very important consideration. Most importantly the *Ko-Hyoteki* could be launched while the submarine was dived since all the restraints and clamps holding it to the casing could be released from within the submarine's control room. In any other navy for the parent submarine to surface to launch a midget submarine was always the most vulnerable moment of any operation.

It was this employment of submarines as carriers which finally won Admiral Yamamoto over. At a series of staff conferences onboard the fleet flagship, *Nagato*, between 11 and 13 October Yamamoto gave his permission for the *Ko-Hyoteki* to take part in the attack on Pearl Harbor – indeed they would spearhead it. Thus in the space of eight months the role of the *Ko-Hyoteki* had totally changed: from ocean-going equaliser to harbour penetration.

As harbour assault craft the *Ko-Hyoteki* were less than successful. Five were deployed in advance of the Japanese attack on Pearl Harbor on 7 December 1941. The deployment of the craft was extremely successful and just after midnight all five were lying off the entrance to Pearl Harbor. Thereafter the story becomes extremely muddled. One was definitely sunk just after 6.00am by the destroyer *Ward* while another was rammed by the destroyer *Monaghan* inside the harbour and a third sunk by the destroyer *Blue*. One of these was commanded by Lieutenant Iwasa Naoji, for shortly after the attack the sleeve of a Japanese naval officer's jacket, laced for a Lieutenant, was recovered from the harbour and Iwasa was the only full Lieutenant in the attack force. The fourth was found by divers off Diamond Head in 1956. Both hatches were open indicating perhaps that the craft had been abandoned after becoming unserviceable. The fifth was driven aground near Bellows Field. The commanding officer, Ensign Sakamki Kazuo, became America's first Japanese prisoner of war. There is no indication as to whether the two *Ko-Hyoteki* which managed to enter the harbour scored any hits on US warships. In all the chaos surrounding the air attack there was no indication was whether a torpedo that found its mark came from an aircraft or a *Ko-Hyoteki*. We shall never know.

Subsequent operations by *Ko-Hyoteki* in the harbour penetration role showed the limitations of the craft when engaged in this sort of operation. At Sydney on 31 May 1942 four craft were sent in to attack the harbour and all were lost. In return an old Sydney harbour ferry, the *Kuttabul*, being used as an accommodation ship was sunk solely because she got in the way of a torpedo. However, twelve hours earlier at Diego Suarez Lieutenant Akeida Saburo successfully entered the harbour and put one torpedo into the British battleship *Ramillies* and another into the tanker *British Loyalty*. Akeida and his crewman were subsequently killed and the other two *Ko-Hyoteki* launched in the operation were sunk.

For the remainder of the war *Ko-Hyoteki* were employed at Guadalcanal, in the Aleutians, the Philippines, off Saipan and at Okinawa without success. Eight were lost off Guadalcanal, three were lost at the Aleutians, eight at the Philippines and five at Saipan. At Okinawa at least ten were destroyed although it is extremely difficult to be sure of the exact number deployed or destroyed. The only time a *Ko-Hyoteki* came close to achieving a significant success was when *No.82* attacked the American cruiser *Boise* as the ship was passing through the Mindanao Sea heading for the Lingayen Gulf and the invasion of Luzon. To sink a cruiser would have been achievement enough, but on this case *Boise* was carrying General Douglas Macarthur and his staff. The *Ko-Hyoteki* fired both torpedoes, the tracks of which were spotted by the USS *Phoenix*. Prompt evasive action by *Boise* saved the ship – and Macarthur – while the *Ko-Hyoteki* was rammed and sunk by the destroyer *David W Taylor*.

Why did the *Ko-Hyoteki* have so little success? The answer is twofold. Firstly, their crews were hopelessly inexperienced. The most seasoned *Ko-Hyoteki* operators had been killed at Pearl Harbor, Diego Suarez and Sydney and there was no pool of operational experience in war or peace for the new men to draw on. Secondly, the *Ko-Hyoteki* were acutely vulnerable to the comprehensive measures deployed against them by the Americans. However gallant their crews were, they were no match for an enemy which enjoyed superiority in almost every field. The effectiveness of the *Ko-Hyoteki* was compromised when their original role was substituted for that of a covert attack weapon. The torpedo is never the best weapon for a craft operating covertly, since the craft has to compromise its position by coming near the surface in order to aim the weapon. Who knows how effective the *Ko-Hyoteki* would have been if used as their designers had intended? At the very least they would have given the opposing fleet commander a good deal to worry about. The *Ko-Hyoteki* was a craft of excellent design and construction, manned by very brave men, but whose operational deployment was not suitable for the craft.

The British *X-Craft*

Genesis of the design

There was no doubt that the *X-Craft* was the most potent and effective of all midget submarines employed during the Second World War. Though it lacked the technical sophistication of the Japanese *Ko-Hyoteki* and the Italian CB craft, this was more than compensated for by its versatility. A brief summary will show the many uses to which the *X-Craft* could be put: attacks against targets in defended harbours, attacks against the enemy's strategic communications, beach reconnaissance, and navigational beacons. Had the war lasted longer, who can say what other uses would have been found for them? Before proceeding to discuss the many and varied operations in which *X-Craft* craft were employed, some discussion of their design, construction and *modus operandi* would be of interest.

It is not true to say that the *X-Craft* was the Royal Navy's first foray into the midget submarine field.

During and after the First World War a plan was proposed for a small craft called the *Devastator* conceived by a British submariner Lieutenant Godfrey Herbert RN. Little is known about *Devastator* largely because much of the discussion concerning her design probably took place across the wardroom bar at HMS *Dolphin*, the British submarine base at Gosport, and thus went unrecorded. All that is known for certain was that she was small and was capable of delivering a 1-ton explosive charge. *Devastator*s were to be used as part of the great fleet engagement which dominated naval thinking during the Great War. They would be carried by capital ships and launched into the water in great numbers just before the two fleets came within gun range.

The *Devastor* was not officially a suicide weapon although the survival chances for its operator were not high! The operator, sitting in a detachable buoyant compartment, set the craft on its course and then released a clip which ejected the compartment by means of compressed air, leaving the rest of the craft

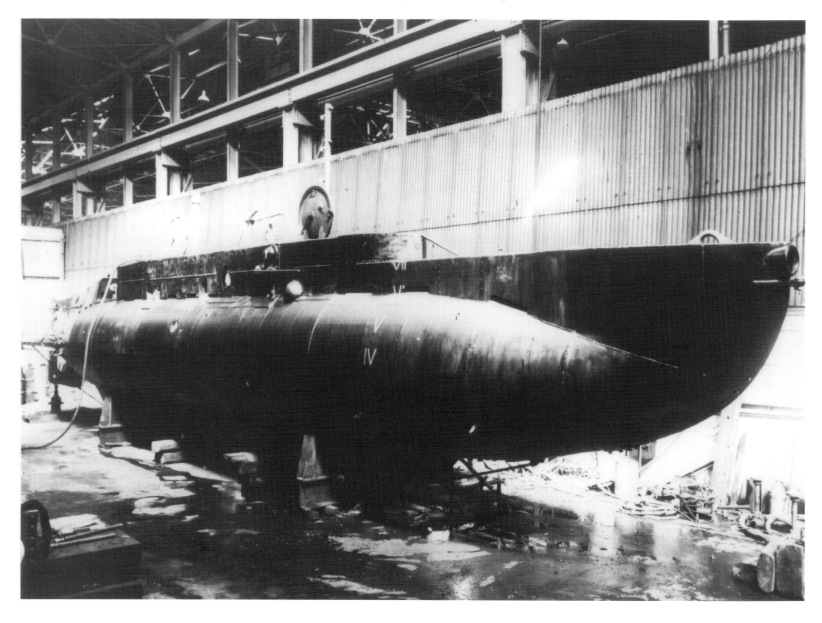

A British *X-Craft* photographed while under construction. (Royal Navy Submarine Museum 0231)

and warhead to proceed to their end. Hopefully a destroyer, tasked for the purpose, would then appear to hoist the chamber and operator aboard. It was a fantastic proposal and one which was wholly unworkable. Nevertheless in 1923 the proposal was given a new lease of life by Captain Max Horton, then Captain (S) of the 2nd Submarine Flotilla. Horton had been an enthusiastic collaborator of Herbert's on the original *Devastator* project and probably nursed the notion of riding the machine himself. But the proposal was turned down for any number of reasons: expense, the innate conservatism of an organisation still firmly wedded to the big gun and the sheer impracticality of the idea. Whether or not the *Devastator* acted as an inspiration for the Japanese *Ko-Hyoteki* is another matter. Britain and Japan were still in the last throes of the Anglo-Japanese alliance, and Japanese naval officers were still accepted on courses in this country. A pencilled note on Horton's paper by an officer on C-in-C Portsmouth's staff remarked, 'This paper is not marked Secret'. Although there is no direct evidence for the link, there is every possibility that the Japanese got wind of Horton's proposal, for the *Ko-Hyoteki* concept mirrored the *Devastator* in a number of ways.

Ironically it was the Army which next pushed Britain into the field of midget submarine development, having ideas for using such a craft to mine the River Rhine. The work passed to the Admiralty following the fall of France and in 1940,[9] the War Office agreed to lend the services of Major Millis Jefferis MC who had produced the original idea to assist in the establishment of a Staff Requirement for the craft. This was defined as a small submarine capable of laying a magnetic mine in shallow and confined waters where more conventional means of minelaying were not appropriate. At the beginning of the project an important principle was established. Though an immensely secret project, the craft would be built under the supervision of the Director of Naval Construction to ensure that it complied fully with constructional standards and requirements. This would not be a covert project carried out by individuals where enthusiasm took precedence over reality. From the beginning *X-Craft* would be part of the Royal Navy's Submarine Service.

The project was first known as 'Job 82' and the first two prototype craft were given the Dockyard job numbers D.235 and D.236. The project was under the supervision of Commander C H Varley DSC RN, a retired submariner, who possessed access to engineering facilities at his own Varley-Marine Works near Southampton, and Commander T I S Bell RN. Varley had already long been interested in midget submarines and human torpedoes, so his appointment was a fortuitous one. He was a larger-than-life personality of whom it was written:

'Crom' Varley was a typical naval officer of the best type, and readily identified as such without the aid of uniform, by his breeziness, geniality and good natured consideration for others. He easily became the centre of any company in which he found himself. He had a great deal of the forthrightness of his ancestor the Lord Protector, while he conspicuously lacked the less attractive characteristics of that great man.[10]

As the design progressed the submarines became known, almost by accident as *X-Craft*. As there had already been an *X.1* and *X.2* in the Royal Navy it was decided that the two prototypes should be numbered *X3* and *X4*. Very many changes were made from the Army design but in March 1942 *X3* was ready for trials swiftly followed by *X4*.

X, XT and XE Craft

In terms of general appearance the craft resembled the early Holland craft which had been the first true submarines in the Royal Navy. Owing to the secrecy under which the craft were built, and different builders being used for *X3* and *X4*, there were minor differences between the prototypes, but these were not more than cosmetic. *X3* and *X4* were never used operationally, instead rendering long and valuable service for trials and experiments of all kinds and at the same time providing early and essential training of personnel. Finally their hulls were surrendered to the Ship Target Trials Committee (STTC) at the end of 1944 for a Promethean end.

The results of the early trials with *X3* and *X4* were very encouraging and the design of the production craft now had to be finalised. The main requirements were for a vessel similar to *X3* with a surface speed of 6kts, a dived speed of 5kts and an endurance of 80 miles at 2kts. The craft had to be able to carry two 4-ton side charges together with sufficient food and water to last the crew for 10 days. The craft also had to be fitted with appropriate towing arrangements since intelligence indicated that German patrols and air reconnaissance would preclude launching the craft from a depot ship off the Norwegian coast as had originally envisaged. However, when asked to produce the sketch design resulting from this requirement, the submarine section of the Directorate of Naval Construction indicated that they were fully occupied with conventional submarine matters and so the work was given to the design section of Vickers at Barrow. This was approved in July 1942 and an order placed for twelve craft.

The *X-Craft* were, of course, intended for use against the *Tirpitz*, safe in her Norwegian lair. For a successful attack certain conditions of moon and hours of darkness were required, conditions which occurred only twice a year. Since the Admiralty wanted to use the *X-Craft* against the *Tirpitz* in March

The 'commissioning' of *X21* at Broadbent's Grantham factory in 1943. *X21* spent all of her service undertaking equipment trials and acting as a 'loyal opposition' for ASW forces. (Royal Navy Submarine Museum 0236)

1943, Vickers were asked to employ all their skill, facilities and experience to ensure that at least six craft were delivered as soon as possible to form the 12th Submarine Flotilla based at HMS *Varbel*[11] at Port Bannatyne on the Isle of Bute. At the same time the contract for the second six was placed with the Broadbent Group of engineering firms.

Vickers were as good as their word. The first boat, *X5*, was laid down in September 1942 and the last, *X10*, was delivered in January 1943. This, given the strained circumstances of Britain's wartime economy, was a remarkable achievement and especially so because at the time Vickers was being criticised by the Admiralty over long delivery times for submarine construction.[12] All five craft were transported by rail from Barrow to Faslane on the Clyde from where a floating dock took the craft in one lift to Port Bannatyne. There the craft and their crews embarked on a period of intensive training. However, the timescale was simply too tight for an attack to be mounted in March so it was put back to September.

The craft ordered from Broadbent were numbered *X20* to *X25* and incorporated experience gained in the construction and trials of the *X5* series. This caused some delay in their production and it was not until the autumn of 1943 that the first of the craft were ready. After the twelve operational craft had been ordered Admiral Horton proposed that a non-operational type of *X-Craft* be built for training purposes and to free the number of submarines employed as anti-submarine targets for operational duties. Originally known as *Z-Craft*, they were subsequently reclassified as *XT-Craft*. Lieutenant H P Westmacott (who commanded *XT5* and later *X24* in Operation 'Heckle') wrote:

> The XT craft was an ideal craft for the purpose of training new entry personnel. The hulls were exactly the same as the X20 boats, the only operational boats in the flotilla . . . Lacking the more complicated equipment they were easier to maintain.[13]

In May 1943 orders for six such craft were placed with Vickers and for twelve craft with Broadbent. The Vickers boats, *XT1* to *XT6*, were delivered by March

Table 15: *X-Craft* series technical particulars

	X3	X4	X5-X10 series	X20 series	XT series	XE series
LENGTH:	43ft 6in	45ft	51ft 7in	51ft 7in	51ft 4in	53ft 1in
BEAM:	5ft 6in	5ft 6in	5ft 9in	5ft 9in	5ft 9in	5ft 9in
DRAUGHT (fwd):	5ft 1in	5ft 1in	5ft 3in	5ft 3in	5ft 9in	5ft 9in
DISPLACEMENT (surface):	22 tons	23 tons	27 tons	26.8 tons	26.5 tons	30.3 tons
(dived):	24 tons	25 tons	29.7 tons	29.8 tons	29.6 tons	33.6 tons
WEIGHT OF SIDE CARGO:	4 tons	4 tons	4 tons	4 tons	Not fitted	4.8 tons
EXPLOSIVE CHARGE:	4480lb	4480lb	4480lb	4700lb	Not fitted	3700lb
SPEED (surface max):	6kts	6kts	6.25kts	6.25kts	6kts	6.6kts
ENDURANCE (at 4.5kts):	1400nm	1300nm	1860nm	1860nm	500nm	1350nm
SPEED (dived max):	5kts	5kts	5.75kts	5.75 kts	5kts	6.09kts
ENDURANCE @ 2kts:	85nm	85nm	82nm	82nm	80nm	88nm
PRESSURE HULL:	8lb	8lb	10lb 'S' steel	10lb	10lb	10lb
OPERATIONAL DIVING DEPTH:	200ft	200ft	300ft	300ft	300ft	300ft
NO OF HATCHES:	1	1	1	1	1	1
BUILDERS:	Varley Marine	HM Dockyard Portsmouth	Vickers, Barrow		See Table 16	
ENGINE MAKERS:	Gardner	Gardner	Gardner	Gardner	Gardner	Gardner
BHP (at 1800rpm):	32	32	42	32	32	42
MAIN MOTOR MAKERS:	Keith Blackman	Keith Blackman	Keith Blackman	Keith Blackman	Keith Blackman	Keith Blackman
HP (at 1650rpm):	32	32	30	30	30	30
TYPE OF BATTERY CELL:	Ediswan	DP BSV/A	Exide 20SP	Exide J380	Exide J380	Exide J418
NO OF CELLS:	96	106	112	112	112	112
CAPACITY AT 5HR RATE:	350 amp hrs	370 amp hrs	440 amp hrs	440 amp hrs	440 amp hrs	484 amp hrs
GYRO COMPASS:	Browns A	Browns A	Browns A	Browns A	Not fitted	Browns A
AUTO HELMSMAN:	Browns	Browns	Browns	Not fitted	Not fitted	Not fitted
MAGNETIC COMPASS:	Not fitted	ACO Mk.XX	ACO Mk.XX	Not fitted	ACO Mk.XX1	ACO Mk.XX11
DIRECTION INDICATOR:	Not fitted	AFV 6A/602	AFV 6A/602	Not fitted	AFV 6A/602	AFV 6A/602
COMPLEMENT:	3	3	4	4	3	4

British *X-Craft* midget submarine.

1944 and were usefully employed as 'targets' in anti-submarine exercises for coastal forces at HMS *Seahawk*, at Loch Fynne where two craft at a time were employed for over a year. *XT*s were also based at Campbeltown, Portsmouth and Harwich. The experience gained in working with the *XT*s was of tremendous value when the Royal Navy had to deal with the menace posed by German midgets in the English Channel following the Normandy landings. The twelve *XT*s, *XT*7 to *XT19* less *XT13*, ordered from

Broadbent were all cancelled. Six were cancelled in March 1944 to be replaced by *XE* craft while the final six were cancelled in September 1944 when it became clear that the six *XT*s already in commission were sufficient to training purposes. The *XT* craft differed substantially from the operational craft. No cargo release gear or night periscope was fitted while the induction mast, which could be lowered in the operational craft, was made a fixed structure.

The final development of the type was the *XE* class.

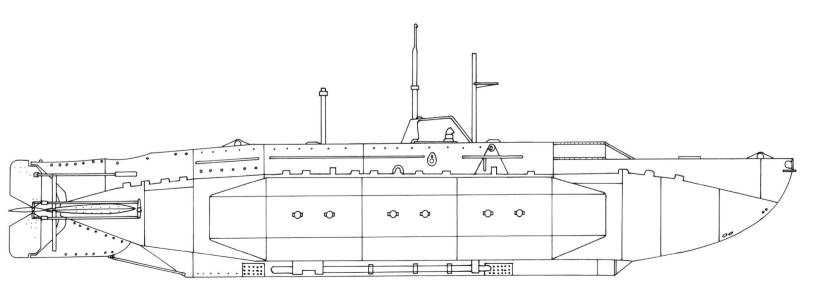

An *XE* series craft being hoisted off her blocks on the depot ship *Bonaventure* in the Far East. The photograph shows the distinctive flat casing of the *XE*s and the induction mast folded down against the hull. (Author)

These were intended for operations in the Far East and thus considerable attention had to be paid to habitability, a feature which had received scant attention in the *X* and *XT* series. Particular attention was also paid to the electrical installation given that conditions in the Far East would be extremely humid. Eighteen *XE* craft were ordered in early 1944: *XE1* to 6 from Vickers and *XE7* to *19* (excluding *13*) from Broadbents. At the end of the year the Vickers six were ready and formed the 14th Submarine Flotilla. After working-up, they then departing for the Far East with their depot ship HMS *Bonaventure* – their subsequent adventures are covered below. Only five, *XE7*, *8*, *9*, *11* and *12* of the Broadbent craft were delivered before the end of the war caused the cancellation of the rest. Of these *XE11* was returned to Broadbents for virtual reconstruction after being rammed by a boom defence vessel and was subsequently broken up. The remainder saw extensive and varied peacetime service before being replaced by the post-war *X51* class.

Design and construction

The operational and *XT* boats were of all welded construction using 10lb 'S' steel. Although there was a nominal diving depth of 300ft, post-war trials using one of the *X20* series showed that the hull did not collapse until the craft had reached nearly 600ft.[14] The hull was constructed in three sections, bolted together

Lieutenant J E Smart RNVR emerging from *X25*'s 'Wet and Dry' compartment. Behind him is the raised induction mast with safety rail and a leather strap which the OOW could use to secure himself to the mast. An alternative position was for the OOW to stand in the 'Wet and Dry' with only his head and shoulders sticking out of the hatch. (Royal Navy Submarine Museum 1344)

internally through flanges. The central section was cylindrical in form, the bow and stern sections conical, and this meant that the craft could be parted on the occasion of a major refit or the replacement of a main engine or motor. Depot ships and shore bases supporting *X-Craft* would carry a complete spare stern section for rapid replacement while the defective section was being repaired. Otherwise there was no need for the craft to be parted since all other equipment could be removed/maintained by use of the existing hatches.

In such a small craft the efficient running and safety of the electrical installation was of major importance. In such a confined space the main battery was far more likely to produce dangerous levels of hydrogen than in a larger submarine. In the prototype craft the battery consisted of 96 individual cells which were stowed in two layers, requiring individual ventilation. A catalyst system was designed by the Admiralty chemist in Portsmouth Dockyard and proved so efficient that it was fitted to all subsequent classes. The battery exhaust gas was first passed through a container of soda lime and charcoal to remove the acid and then through a heated catalyst of palladised asbestos. Subsequent trials and operational experience showed that the hydrogen concentrations never rose above 0.8 per cent – a very safe figure. In *X5* and subsequent classes the battery was stowed forward with general ventilation arrangements, though the same catalyst system was fitted. One hundred and twelve Exide J.380 cells were fitted in the *X* and *XT* craft while the *XE* craft had the same number of J.418 Exide cells which were designed for the higher temperatures found in the Far East.

Table 16: Career details of *X5*, *X20*, *XT* and *XE* series craft

X5	Built Vickers 1942, sunk *c*22 Sep 1943 during Operation 'Source'.
X6	Built Vickers 1942, scuttled 22 Sep 1943 after placing side cargoes beneath *Tirpitz*.
X7	Details as *X6*.
X8	Built Vickers 1942, abandoned 16 Sep 1943 during outward passage on Operation 'Source'.
X9	Built Vickers 1942, foundered 16 Sep 1943 as a result of broken tow rope during outward passage on Operation 'Source'.
X10	Built Vickers 1942, scuttled 23 Sep 1943 after Operation 'Source'.
X20	Built Broadbent 1943, extant until Oct 1945.
X21	Built Broadbent 1943, extant until Oct 1945.
X22	Built Markham 1943, rammed and sunk by HMS/M *Syrtis* 7 Feb 1944.
X23	Built Markham 1943, extant until Jul 1945.
X24	Built Marshall 1943, preserved at the Royal Navy Submarine Museum.
X25	Built Marshall, extant until Oct 1945.
XT1-6	Built Vickers 1943-44, extant until Oct 1945
XT7-19	Built Broadbent, cancelled 1944.
XE1-6	Built Vickers, broken up in Australia, 1945.
XE7-8	Built Broadbent. *XE7* BU 1952. *XE8* preserved at Imperial War Museum.
XE9-10	Built Marshall. *XE9* BU 1952. *XE10* cancelled.
XE11	Built Markham. Rammed and sunk 6 Mar 1945. Salved and BU.
XE12	Built Markham. BU 1952.

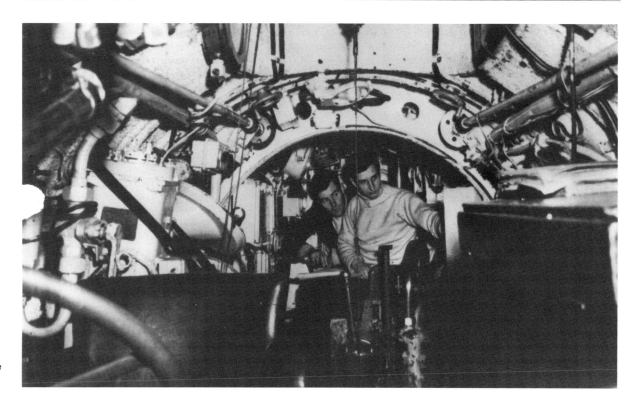

A view of the cramped control room of an *X-Craft*. (Royal Navy Submarine Museum 0238)

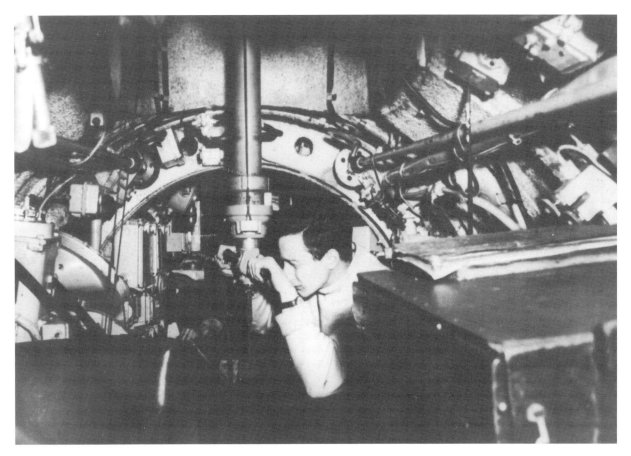

An officer using the periscope of an *X-Craft*. (Royal Navy Submarine Museum 0241)

Carbon dioxide exhaled by the crew was absorbed by Protosorb. In the prototypes, Protosorb trays were simply left on the deck but this was found to be too cumbersome and awkward in such small craft. In the *X* and *XT* classes Protosorb was carried in 6lb canisters which were placed in the ventilation trunking, while in the *XE* class 10lb canisters were carried. Oxygen was carried in cylinders–*XE*s carried three cylinders, totalling 4.5ft^3, in the control room, the air being released when required through a control valve.

The *X-Craft* used conventional diesel propulsion when on the surface and electric drive when dived. The diesel engine, either a 32bhp or 42bhp Gardner diesel, mounted on a sound-insulated raft, proved exceptionally reliable. The engine was the same as used in a London bus and proved just as reliable running up a Norwegian fjord as it did running along the Embankment. The engine naturally had to be adapted for marine use and was fitted with a fresh-water cooling system which in the *XE* craft could be topped up from the Freon distillate tank. If the fresh-water cooling system failed it was possible to use seawater from the Wet and Dry (W&D) compartment. Air was drawn down to the engine by means of a folding induction mast (although this was a fixed structure in the *XT* class) while the exhaust gasses were expelled by a muffled drowned exhaust. The main motor, of conventional design, developed from the open 30hp Keith Blackman motor fitted to *X3* to the fully enclosed water-cooled model designed by Metro-

Vickers for the *XE* class. The switch gear was of the drum type and was specially proofed against damp.

The control systems replicated those of a conventional submarine in miniature. Since there was only a small crew only one set of hydroplanes was fitted at the stern in order to save space and weight. The prototypes experienced some problems in submerged control which were investigated in the Admiralty

Internal view of the control room of an *X-Craft* looking aft. On the left is the helmsman while behind him is the first lieutenant at the diving controls. (Royal Navy Submarine Museum 0232)

A view over the helmsman's shoulder showing the gyro repeater. The hatch to his left leads forward into the 'Wet and Dry' and then the battery space. (Royal Navy Submarine Museum 1091)

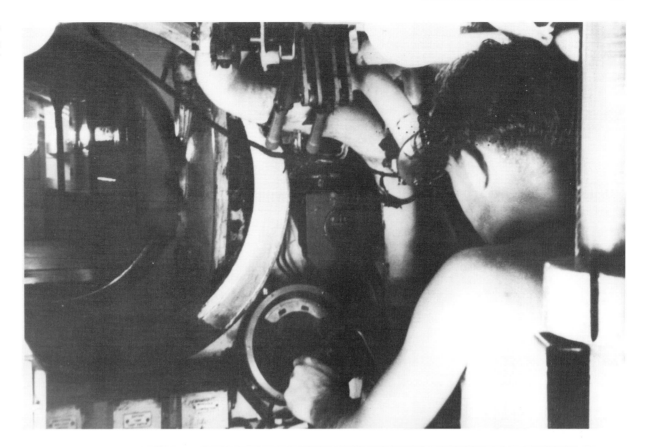

Sub-Lieutenant 'Robbie' Robertson RNVR at the diving controls of an *XT-Craft*. The large wheel at the left hand corner of the photograph is the release wheel for the side cargoes. (Royal Navy Submarine Museum 0239)

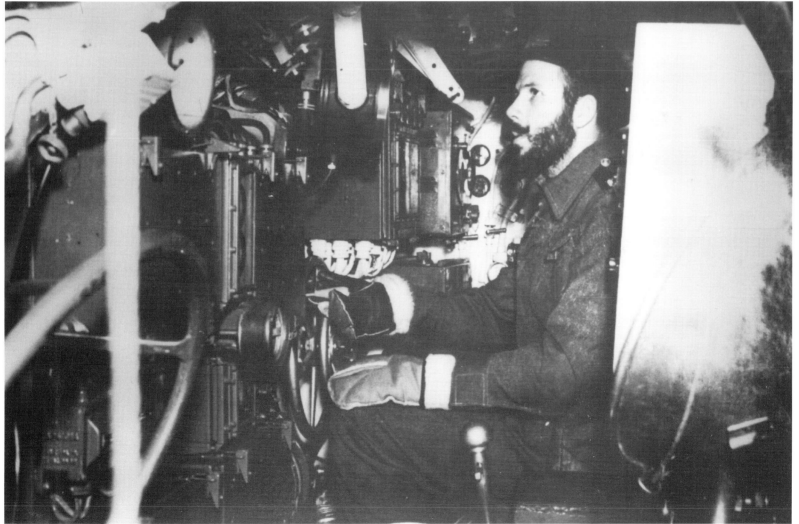

Experimental Tank at Haslar. These showed that with only one screw fitted, the hydroplanes lacked sufficient power to control the craft. The solution was to extend the surface of the hydroplane aft so that the rudder had to split into upper and lower sections in order to allow both to benefit from the slipstream. Initially power-operated steering was fitted with emergency hand steering. But the power steering was removed in the *X20* class for buoyancy reasons – the hand steering gear was found to be so effective that it was retained. Despite the elementary nature of the *X-Craft*'s controls, they handled very well when dived. As the Technical Monograph on the *X-Craft* noted:

> Whereas the orthodox submarine cannot do more than hold a stopped trim in certain favourable circumstances, *X-Craft* could be manoeuvred astern submerged, backed and filled and raised or lowered while stopped without difficulty by a skilful crew. This attribute was of the greatest advantage when the technique of accurately laying the charges beneath the target was developed.[15]

The *X-Craft* possessed navigational instruments of considerable sophistication, given their small size. A gyro compass was fitted since it was considered that it was impossible to position a magnetic compass far enough away from the hull to ensure sufficient accuracy. The gyros gave endless trouble: three of the six craft engaged in Operation 'Source' suffered gyro failure, while *X24*'s gyro gave out on both her operations against targets at Bergen. In the second raid, Operation 'Heckle', *X24* was proceeding up the Hjeltefjord with her gyro in pieces in the control room being reassembled by a very harassed ERA.

A magnetic compass was subsequently fitted outside the hull in the top of a periscopic pinnacle, an image of which was projected onto a screen in front of the helmsman. In the operational *X-Craft* the binnacle, Type ACO Mk.XX, could be raised and lowered as required, but in the training *XT* series, the binnacle, the Mk.XXI, was fixed in the 'up' position. For the *XE* series a more sophisticated version was produced, the Mk.XXII, which included compensating arrangements for the degaussing equipment. Although the magnetic compass was a satisfactory back-up under normal conditions, it was totally useless during the form of attack in which the *X-Craft* specialised: harbour penetration. The raised binnacle was likely to become fouled on nets, it took too long to raise and activate if the gyro compass failed and was liable to damage while the *X-Craft* was manoeuvring under the target. Even if all man-made hazards failed to upset the compass, it was found that the distortion in the Earth's magnetic field caused by the presence of the target was sufficient to send it completely haywire. It was therefore necessary to find some non-magnetic

A view of the port side of an *X-Craft* showing the air induction mast, used when the boat was running on the surface to supply the 42bhp diesel engine with air. It also doubled as a voice pipe. In operational *X* and *XE* craft it was a hinged structure which folded down against the side of the hull when not in use. However in the *XT* series, it was a fixed mast. The mast was provided with a safety rail, known as the Hezlet safety rail after Commander Arthur Hezlet, for the OOW to hold onto. Just behind the mast is the non-elevating night periscope used when on the surface at night or for checking that the diver is clear of the Wet and Dry. Behind the night periscope the boat's normal periscope can be seen in the raised position. (Royal Navy Submarine Museum 0240)

means of navigation for this phase of the operation. A variety of mechanical direction indicators were evaluated and eventually an Air Ministry Model, AFV 6A/602, was chosen. This could be pre-set either by eye or from the gyro and was liable to a maximum 'wander' of 5 degrees either side of the set course in 20 minutes. It was not, therefore, especially accurate, but sufficient for what was required. However, on one occasion, when the device was most needed, it malfunctioned with potentially disastrous consequences. *X10* (Lt K Hudspeth RANVR) was retiring down Altenfjord following her commanding officer's decision to abandon the attack on *Scharnhorst* during Operation 'Source', and both the gyro and magnetic compasses were wandering. Hudspeth decided to dive and use the Direction Indicator. However, on surfacing for a routine 'guff through' they found the device had turned the craft through 180° and that they were headed *back up* the fjord.

While the *X-Craft* was making its submerged run-in toward the target it was, naturally, 'blind' since periscope observation of the target would be impossible. In an effort to improve navigation during this most important part of the operation, two blind navigation devices were tested but eventually discarded. The first was a 'Course Indicator' which consisted of a long, hinged, flexible arm which was stowed alongside the keel but could be lowered so that it rested on the bottom. Riding on a hinge and pivoted so that it showed the deviation from a fore and aft line on a pointer inside the craft, it was designed to show the true course made good over the ground. Fitted along this device was a taut wire measuring device consisting of 20 miles of special fine wire wound onto a bobbin to give the actual distance run along the bottom. Both devices were fine in theory but in practice it was found that they caused the navigator far more work than their results justified and although they had been fitted to *X5* to *X10*, they were removed before Operation 'Source'. Other navigational aids consisted of a cherikeff log and an echo sounder, described later. A small chart table was fitted although cramped conditions in the *X-Craft* meant that the chart always had

The engine room of an *XE* series craft taken from the control room. (Royal Navy Submarine Museum 105951)

to be folded and, invariably, the fold always lay in the part of the chart which was being used.

Hydrophones were first fitted to *X-Craft* as a safety measure while the craft were in training, to warn of the approach of any traffic which might have unwittingly entered the training area. This was a sonic tank-type device on either bow which was connected to a switching device so that the operator could either maintain an all-round watch or listen alternately to the port or starboard hydrophones. However, during the trials process it became abundantly clear that something more sophisticated was required. In particular there was a need for a directional hydrophone to monitor the movements of harbour patrol craft so that avoiding action could be taken. The equipment selected was similar to the Type 129 set used in 'conventional' submarines but in order to give the same performance, the diameter was reduced from 15in to 5in while the frequency was increased to 30 kc/s from 10 kc/s. A quartz hydrophone was mounted on and rotated with the night periscope while a simple battery-powered amplifier and headphones completed the installation. In trials in Loch Striven using the prototype *X3*, good bearings within 2° of the day periscope readings were obtained despite the jerky rotation. During practice attacks it was found that the low-frequency noise emanating from the target vessel's auxiliary machinery (which would be running continuously whether or not the vessel in question was under way) could be used by the *X-Craft* as a means of homing-in on the target. The idea seemed fine in principle and a low-frequency hydrophone was developed for this purpose. However, trials of this instrument showed that although a general increase in noise was detected from the vague direction of the target vessel, it was not of a sufficient level to aid navigation and furthermore the hydrophone was extremely susceptible to noise from passing small craft. As these were precisely the conditions under which the set would have to perform in an enemy harbour, the project was abandoned.

The relative failure to use low-frequency sound emanating from the target led to the development of a high-frequency hydrophone which would indicate when the *X-Craft* was directly under the target. Originally it was proposed to simply invert an echo-sounder but this was rejected on the grounds that the impulses would be easily detectable. The Mine Department at the Admiralty then stepped in and proposed the use of a magnetic detector, but it was found in trials with *X3* that the magnetic detector did not give a very definite indication of the precise position of the target, so attention reverted to the hydrophone. To reduce the risk of detection, the impulses from the hydrophone had to be very high – 300 kc/s. This was ten times higher than any known enemy hydrophone could operate and produced such a sharp vertical

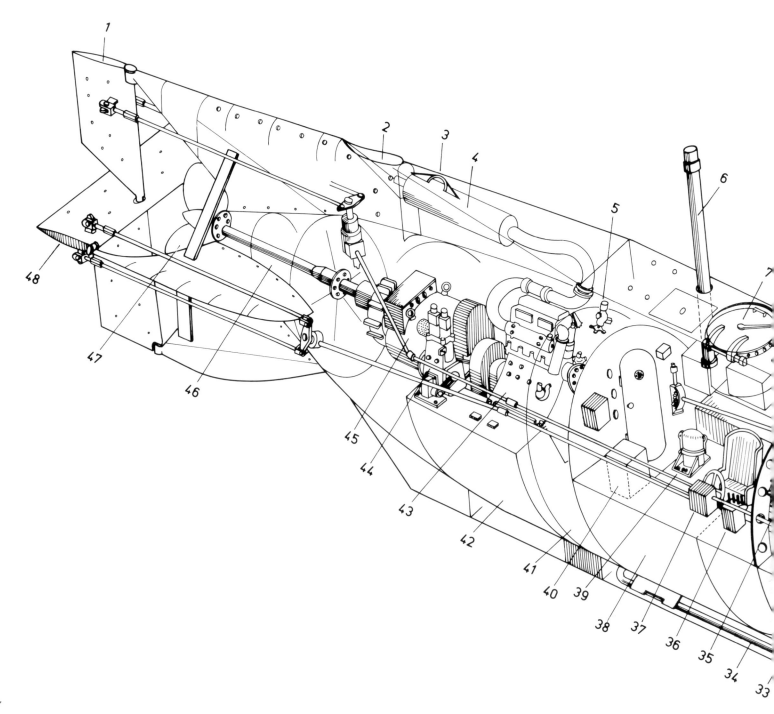

Key

1. Rudder.
2. Exhaust recess.
3. Mooring eye.
4. Diesel exhaust muffler.
5. Fuel oil filling valve.
6. Projection compass.
7. After hatch.
8. Attack periscope.
9. Observation scuttle.
10. Night periscope.
11. Induction mast.
12. Compensation pump.
13. No.2 & No.3 main tank vents.

14. Wet & dry hatch.
15. No.1 main tank vent.
16. No.1 main tank.
17. Mooring eye.
18. Towing cable tube.
19. Mooring eye plate.
20. Free flooding space.
21. Free flooding holes.
22. Forward trim tank.
23. Fuel oil tank.
24. Air bottles.
25. Main battery.
26. Racks for stowage.

27. No.2 main tank (below and around wet & dry compartment).
28. Recess for No.2 and 'Q' kingstons.
29. Helm position,
30. Main vent levers.
31. Quick diving tank.
32. Periscope raising motor.
33. Compensation tank.
34. Degaussing magnet.
35. Side cargo release gear (port & starboard).
36. Engine controls.

37. Combined hydroplane/steering control.
38. No.3 main tank.
39. Log tank.
40. Main motor controller.
41. No.3 tank kingston recess.
42. Fuel oil tank.
43. 4-cylinder Gardner diesel engine.
44. Air compressor.
45. Main motor.
46. After trim tank.
47. Propeller.
48. Hydroplane.

X-Craft General Arrangement

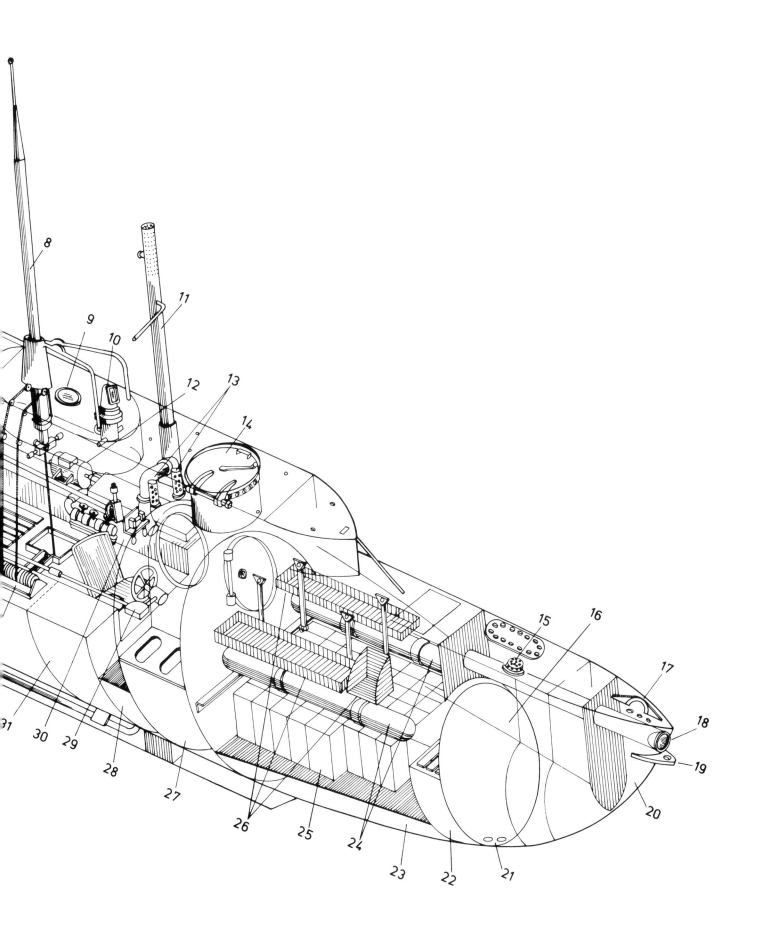

beam that interception was considered highly unlikely. The echoes were displayed on a cathode ray tube and the method had the additional advantage in that it was possible to calculate the draft of the target so that mistakes in attacking shallow-draft vessels could be avoided.

The development of the set, called the Type 151 target indicator, was accorded a high priority and trials took place aboard *X8* in June 1943. Unfortunately no sooner had the device been fitted than *X8* collided with the target vessel and the apparatus was damaged. Subsequently refitted in *X5*, the set gave very good results, proving able to recognise nets and other obstructions as well as the target. Six sets were ordered and fitted in the six craft destined to embark on Operation 'Source'. The quartz oscillator was mounted flush with the casing and protected with a metal grid. The entire installation comprising transmitter, receiver, cathode ray tube, oscillator and pressure hull gland weighed only 53lbs – a masterpiece of miniaturisation. The usefulness of the Type 151 was further extended by fitting a second oscillator face-down in the keel. A selector switch connected either oscillator to the depth meter and this meant that 'soundings' of up to 100ft either way could be obtained.

Experience gained during Operation 'Source' and subsequent operations off the Norwegian coast showed that there was a need for a short-range underwater communication system to be used while the *X-Craft* was being towed, dived, by the parent submarine since the previous method of using a telephone cable secured to the tow-rope had proved unreliable. Furthermore there was a need for communication between the submarine and the *X-Craft* after the tow had been slipped or, for some reason, if the tow parted. The equipment became known as the Type 713 Hydrophone and was based on the submarine's Type 129 asdic in which the set was switched to transmit, the transmission being used as a carrier and modulated by voice. Good speech was received at ranges of up to 1000 yards but if the *X-Craft* was directly astern of the submarine it was found that the sound beam was blanked by her ballast keel. This disadvantage led to the development of the Type 156 underwater telegraphy set, consisting of a combined transmitter and receiver with an oscillator working on 10 kc/s fitted in the forward ballast tank. The parent submarine used her Type 129 set in the normal manner for SST communication. This equipment proved of immense use, particularly in the Far East, when on one occasion the tow broke and the auxiliary tow had to be passed. A special hydrophone set was fitted to *X20* and *X24* which were tasked with the reconnaissance of the invasion beaches in Normandy prior to the D-Day landings in June 1944. These two craft were fitted with a standard small boat echo sounder together with a chemical recorder. This latter had to be carried,

A view looking forward from the 'Wet and Dry' compartment of *X51* into the battery compartment. (Royal Navy Submarine Museum 1240)

despite its considerable bulk, as it was necessary to bring back permanent records for analysis by the invasion planners.

Another feature of the craft was the Wet and Dry Compartment (known as the W&D) whereby a diver could leave and re-enter the craft for the purpose of placing underwater charges, cutting nets or clearing obstructions. The compartment was placed in the centre of the craft, surrounded by No.2 ballast tank, with hatches leading forward into the control room and aft into the engine-room, and the exit hatch leading up onto the casing. To leave the craft underwater the diver entered the W&D, shut the hatches behind him and using a telephone link informed the First Lieutenant that he was ready. The latter then applied LP pressure to the ballast tank, the Kingstons being shut, so that water began to enter the W&D, the displaced air venting into the control room. The LP air was shut off when the compartment was nearly full and the inboard vent shut when water spilled out. While the W&D flooded up the diver was subjected to the slow increase in pressure, an unpleasant sensation grimly known as the 'Squeeze'. Meanwhile the diver opened the equalising cock in the hatch and emerged, shutting the hatch behind him in case he failed to return. Before the diver returned No.2 ballast tank was vented inboard ready for the diver's return.

These arrangements proved satisfactory but cumbersome. In particular the position of the W&D in the centre of the craft made passage from the control room to the engine-room difficult when it was dry and impossible when it was flooded. Consequently in *X5* and subsequent craft, the W&D was placed forward of the control room so that only the battery compartment was isolated. Other improvements included the fitting of a silenced W&D pump to replace the rather noisy LP blower, cross-connected to the compensating pump in case of failure. In the early craft a number of cable runs, ventilation shafts, trunkings and water pipes had to be led through the W&D and the fluctuating air and water pressure played havoc with the glands. In the *XE* series and subsequent craft all these were passed over the top of the W&D. One feature of the W&D remained impervious to all change or modification. It was the only place onboard where the WC could be located. The latter was a cramped, hand-pumped hazardous inconvenience with the ever-present hazard of 'getting ones own back'.[16] The latter phenomenon was bad enough in an ordinary submarine: in an *X-Craft* it was nothing short of catastrophic.

Allied to the role of the diver was the provision of net cutters to allow him to carve a way through net defences. The first net cutters were simple hand-held shears recovered from Italian *Decima MAS* operators captured at Gibraltar, but these were useless against the type of wire mesh nets thought to be protecting *Tirpitz* so something more effective was required. The advice of the director of Boom Defence at the Admiralty was sought and he produced three versions of an air-powered cutter, Mks I, II & III, which though capable of cutting through thick nets was cumbersome to operate, requiring the use of both hands and, being air-powered, left a tell-tale trail of bubbles on the surface. The comparative failure of the air-powered cutter led to the decision that the firm of Starkie Gardner (who made standard net cutters for the Navy) should be informed as to why powerful cutters were required. Though the security officers frowned, it proved a wise decision. Starkie Gardner produced the Mk.IV which was little more than an improved Mk.III except that it could be operated one-handed, before introducing the Mk.V. This was a radical departure in that it was hydraulically-powered, producing no bubbles. Further refinements produced the Mk.VI cutter which was the version finally adopted by the Admiralty. This was a one-handed cutter looking like an outsize tree pruner which could cut through 3.5in steel wire with enough fluid in the reservoir for twenty-two cuts. Two such cutters were carried by each *X-Craft* stored in lockers in the casing. So much work had gone into the design and development of the Mk.VI cutter that it was immediately classified 'Secret'.

The time of entering a net was planned so that the *X-Craft* would be running against the tide. This enabled the captain to manoeuvre the craft at a depth of around 25ft into and through the net while maintaining full submerged control. The diver would then start cutting at the base of the *X-Craft*'s keel, cutting a slit upwards in each successive strand so that the *X-Craft* gradually pushed through. It sounds easy but in the cold waters of a Scottish loch or Norwegian Fjord, it was easy to amputate a finger without noticing the loss–and not just in cold northern waters. During the cutting of the Hong Kong to Singapore underwater telephone cable in 1945 by *XE5* the diver accidentally cut his thumb off. While trying to enter the W&D he became entangled with a Portuguese Man o'War jelly fish and was very badly stung–owing to the ambient water temperature he was not wearing a suit. Eventually he made it back into the W&D and was hauled out and thrown down on the control room deck and given a shot of morphine in his backside, vigorously administered by *XE5*'s commanding officer, Lieutenant H P Westmacott RN. Before the drug took effect he was heard to mutter, 'My God, what next!'.[17]

Given that the Royal Navy paid little attention to the subject of 'acoustic housekeeping' in its submarines, the attention paid to this matter in *X-Craft* was remarkable. At first it was thought that the small size of the *X-Craft* would be its protection, but early trials with the prototypes showed that they were incredibly noisy, resulting in a hasty programme of silencing and noise reduction of all machinery on board. Special attention was paid to the design of the propeller to avoid cavitation and thrash at speeds below 3kts, while singing was avoided by thinning the edges of the propellers. Similar work was done with the reduction system although a supposedly 'silent' chain system fitted in *X21* proved noiser than the exisiting meshed gears and was quickly removed. *XT5* was built 18in longer than her sisters to allow the main motor and diesel to be mounted on a common sound-insulated bed connected to the hull by special clips. The installation proved most successful and was subsequently fitted to the boats of the *XE* class. The one seemingly insoluble acoustic problem was the transmission of pump noise through the water in the system and was only partially solved by the fitting of special filters and flexible pipe connections. Other aspects of acoustic housekeeping included the removal of all unnecessary external fittings.

During trials at the submarine sound range on Loch Goil, conveniently situated near to the *X-Craft* base at Kames Bay, a detectability range of 500 yards was set, and reached, for all machinery used during an attack An idea of the progress made can be gauged by the fact that the *X5* to *X10* class were initially restricted to 1000rpm when within 10,000 yards of the target for fear of cavitation and thrash while a year later *XE5* ran her motors at 1000rpm and was undetectable until she was within 1000 yards. The gyro, battery fan, W&D pump and other machinery could be run with impunity 500 yards from the sensitive hydrophones used for the test.[18] Noise reduction was a continually-

The *XE* series craft, specially built for service in the Far East, are easily distinguished by the fact that there is no break in their casing. This is one of the six *XE-Craft* (*XE1, 2, 3, 4, 5* and *6*) which were sent to the Far East and was photographed in Sydney in early 1946. Note the night periscope and the Hezlet safety rail on the induction mast. (Author)

An *XE* series craft parted for essential maintenance in Sydney Harbour. (Royal Navy Submarine Museum. 3515B)

monitored process. In every depot ship where *X-Craft* were employed special sound-monitoring equipment was embarked together with an officer specifically charged with making sure that each craft was as quiet as possible.

It seemed that no aspect of *X-Craft modus operandi* was beyond the Navy's attention. The advent of radar during the Second World War led to the fear that an *X-Craft* might be thus detected while on the surface. Accordingly the silhouette was kept as low as possible, despite the disadvantages this caused, and early plans to give the craft a collapsible conning tower were quickly shelved. The distinctive 'step' on the casing in the *X* and *XT* classes was removed in the *XE* class since it was found to be very distinctive at night. Furthermore the bow and stern of the *XE* class were rounded down to make them even harder to spot. Camouflage was another matter to which considerable attention was paid. After a number of schemes, including 'Mountbatten Pink' had been tested, it was decided to adopt the standard submarine scheme of grey sides and black upper surfaces although the *XE* class were painted black overall. The only exception to this rule were the two *X-Craft* which operated off the French coast prior to Operation 'Overlord', which were painted yellow ochre, stone and Hooker's green for protection from air observation when operating close to the shore in day time. Other passive defence measures included the fitting of degaussing equipment, net detectors and coating the hull in anti-magnetic paint to counter magnetic indicator nets.

The *X-Craft* lacked sufficient range to reach the target under its own 'steam' so was usually towed part of the way. Towing was not the first method selected but was adopted by force of circumstances when it was realised that no depot ship could approach to within launching range of the target without being detected, thereby losing the advantage of surprise. The favoured option was then to use fishing trawlers and trials were successfully conducted in February 1943 using the *Bergholm*. However, to have the *X-Craft* towed by another submarine was the best method and the 'T' class submarine HMS/M *Tuna* was allocated for trials in March 1943. These trials were successful with *Tuna* towing an *X-Craft* at speeds of up to 10kts, dived and on the surface, without any significant problems of control, the *X-Craft*, in the words of *Tuna*'s commanding officer 'followed like a lamb'.[19]

The question of the tow rope proved an intractable one. Manila was initially selected – 100 fathoms of 4.5in constituted the tow rope into which was woven a telephone cable. However these were prone to break after between 60 and 80 hours of use. Consultation with salvage experts, who had to be fully briefed on the project in order that their expertise could be profitably employed, showed that frequent heavy stresses imposed on the waterlogged tow rope as the *X-Craft* surged up on the tow caused the structure of the rope to disintegrate and that a critical period of 70 hours was reached when under a sudden strain the tow rope would part. Towing trials with *X20* in rough but bright weather showed the *X-Craft* surging forward

HMS/M *Thrasher* tows *X5* out of Loch Cairnbawn on 11 September 1943 to begin operation *Source*. *X5* made a successful passage across the Norwegian Sea but disappeared during the operation. Her fate is unknown. (Author)

on the tow which then curled back like a whiplash over the little submarine. The rope could not be seen as the strain came on, but this undoubtedly the moment when the damage was done.

The alternative was to use a nylon tow rope. The use of nylon for towing purposes had been developed by the Air Ministry in connection with gliders and after some debate, for nylon was a valuable material, the Air Ministry agreed to part with 600lbs. That amount of nylon would make 20,000 pairs of black stockings and a fortune for whoever could dispose of them on the Black Market–hence the Air Ministry's caution! The first test nylon tow rope endured over 3500 miles of towing without appreciable sign of wear and tear. So impressed was he with the nylon rope that Lieutenant Donald Cameron RNVR insisted on having a nylon tow rope for *X7* in Operation 'Source'. His decision was well-founded: *X8* broke her tow *en route* and foundered, probably dragged down by the weight of the sodden rope. So successful was the nylon tow rope that, like the net cutter, its details were immediately classified as 'Secret'.

There was, however, one aspect of the *X-Craft* to which little or no attention was paid and that was habitability. Conditions aboard were unbelievably squalid and could not be endured by anyone who was not wholly dedicated to the task or who had not previously experienced life at a British public school (or Britannia Royal Navy College, Dartmouth). Each *X-Craft* had a crew of four: commanding officer; first lieutenant, engineer and diver. Trials with the craft soon showed it would be beyond the endurance of one crew to take an *X-Craft* across the North Sea, carry out an operation and then return, so accordingly each *X-Craft* was allocated a Passage Crew who would operate it during the outward passage and exchange with operational crew when the tow was slipped. The Passage Crew was the same composition as the operational crew less the diver. The role of the passage crew was unenviable:

Their craft was submerged most of the tow during which they had to make sure everything was on top line for the operational team who would have, naturally, most of the excitement and the rewards.[20]

Bottom left: One evolution which required practice was the change-over between passage and operational crews. This was usually done by dinghy as shown here with four cheerful *X-Craft* men about to rejoin the towing submarine. (Royal Navy Submarine Museum 10595A)

Below: A unusual view of an *X-Craft* from below. This photograph gives a good view of the propeller and control surfaces and shows the side cargoes attached. Note how the shape of the side cargoes is formed to mould in with the boat's hull as much as possible. (Royal Navy Submarine Museum 1789)

Right: A view of one of the side cargoes containing 3750lb of Amatex (Amatol plus 9 per cent RDX). The cargo would be, literally, 'screwed on' to the craft and released by unscrewing the holding bolt by turning a wheel in the control room. (Royal Navy Submarine Museum 5438)

Below: The alternative to the side cargo was carrying a quantity of limpet mines. This photograph of two *XE* series craft onboard HMS *Bonaventure* shows the lockers attached port and starboard in which these mines were stowed. They could then be retrieved by the diver and attached to the victim's hull. (Royal Navy Submarine Museum 5590B)

Right forward in the craft there was a bunk placed on top of the battery cells. Even if the sleepy occupant managed to avoid dragging a hand across the terminals, he was likely to awake with a splitting headache and lungs full of hydrogen. As a result the preferred place for a sleep was on a foreshortened couch in the control room or curled around the periscope. Needless to say there was no galley onboard. A single vessel in the control room served as a cooker. The first four tins which came to hand were emptied into the pot, stirred and heated. Understandably even the hardiest appetite faded after a day or so of 'Potmess'.

The armament of an *X-Craft* initially consisted of two large side charges containing 2 tons each of amatol. However, tests showed that the original amatol charge did not detonate completely although a charge composed of amatex did do so. Furthermore the original casings leaked at depths below 200ft and had to be redesigned. In the final Mk.XX charge (which was made negatively buoyant by the addition of free-flooding ballast chambers so that it would sink and not embarrassingly bob to the surface), the total weight of the charge was 5.5 tons of which 3700lbs constituted the minol charge with a 10 per cent cyclonite addition. The charges would be laid directly below the target and fitted with a variable time fuse to allow the *X-Craft* to clear the area. *X-Craft* could also carry limpet mines stowed in the casing which could be planted on the target's hull by the diver. In order to keep the *X-Craft* stationary while the diver placed the mines, all *X-Craft* from the *XE* series on were fitted with three special hinged, spring-loaded antennae which could be raised from within the craft. Once the *X-Craft* was beneath the target, the antennae were raised and then slight positive buoyancy was applied so that the craft rose gently upwards until it rested securely against the target's hull. The antennae left sufficient room for the diver to leave and re-enter the W&D.

After placing the charges or mines, the *X-Craft* would clear the area as quickly as possible. The risk of

Above: X5 onboard the depot ship HMS *Bonaventure* before the attack on the *Tirpitz* in September 1943. (Royal Navy Submarine Museum 0293)

X24 at loch Cairnbawn flying her 'Jolly Roger' after a successful mission to Bergen under the command of Lieutenant Max Shean RANVR on 13 April 1944 in which the merchant ship *Barenfels* was sunk. However, Shean's intended target had been the nearby floating dock so in September 1944 Lieutenant Percy Westmacott took *X24* back to Bergen to complete the job. (Author)

X23, commanded by Lieutenant George Honour RNR, returns to the depot ship *Largs* on 6 June 1944 having, together with *X20*, preceded the D-Day invasion fleet by some 24 hours in order to act as a navigational beacon for landing craft headed toward 'Juno' and 'Sword' beaches. (Author)

detection increased with time and it was unwise to remain when the side cargoes or limpets detonated. There then remained the long journey out to the rendezvous with the parent submarine, the exchange of recognition signals and the welcome appearance of the passage crew for the return journey.

That then was the *X-Craft* – a most potent weapon of war. There are two points of specific interest when considering its design. Firstly, the craft was an integral part of the submarine service and its construction and equipment were based on sound submarine practice rather than the enthusiasm of a Special Forces establishment. Secondly, as in the case of the tow rope and the net cutter, the Admiralty were prepared to risk compromising the programme by enlisting the best advice available – even from civilian contractors. This is an important point which applies to all such craft and which is not generally appreciated.

X-Craft operations

X-Craft operations were a remarkable synthesis of planning from all areas of Britain's armed and intelligence services. Purely naval planning was supplemented by air reconnaissance from the RAF and intelligence from the SIS and SOE. The latter organisation also supplied details of Partisan or Resistance liaison in countries such as Norway and Malaysia where such organisations existed. *X-Craft* crews were certainly the best-prepared out of all the midget submarine operators and the care taken in the organisation of their operations did not go unnoticed. In his report on Operation 'Heckle' Lieutenant Westmacott wrote:

> . . . my thanks to the Norwegian officer who instructed us in evasion. The trust he placed in us by giving us the information he did was felt to be a compliment beyond words. [21]

X-Craft operations were also highly selective. Unlike the German midget submarines, and the use of the Japanese *Ko-Hyoteki* in the later stages of the war,

Table 17: *X-Craft* operations

Date	X-Craft Involved	Code Name	Target	Losses
22 Sep '43	*X5-X10*	'Source'	*Tirpitz*	All 6 craft
17-21 Jan '44	*X20*	'Postage Able'	Normandy beach reconnaissance	None
13 Apr '44	*X24*	'Guidance'	Floating dock, Bergen	None
2-5 Jun '44	*X20* & *X23*	'Gambit'	Navigational beacon for invasion force	None
11 Sept '44	*X24*	'Heckle'	Floating dock, Bergen	None
31 Jul '45	*XE1* & *XE3*	'Struggle'	Jap. Cruiser *Takao*	None
31 Jul '45	*XE4*		Saigon-Hong Kong & Saigon-Singapore telephone cables	None
31 Jul '45	*XE5*		Hong-Kong-Singapore telephone cable	None

A highly decorated group of *X-Craft* personnel taken after the war. From left to right: Lieutenant L K 'Buster' Crabbe OBE GM; Lieutenant B G Place VC DSC RN (commander of *X7* in Operation 'Source'); Leading Seaman J Magennis VC (*XE3*'s diver awarded the VC for the attack on the *Takao*); Tom Waldron; Lieutenant Ian Fraser VC DSC RNR (commander of *XE3* in the attack on the *Takao*); James Gleeson and Lieutenant Commander Donald Cameron VC RNR (commander of *X6* in Operation 'Source'). (Royal Navy Submarine Museum.0727)

X-Craft were never simply sent to sea in the hope of sinking something. Their operations were always directed to a specific end, and thus it is easy to make a record of them (Table 17).

In terms of results these operations are quite impressive – certainly the most successful of any of the craft described in this book. Those successes can be ascribed to the right craft, coupled with specific and directed operational planning and highly-trained personnel. Operation 'Source' is the best known of these operations. Of the six *X-Craft* deployed two (*X8* and *X9*) were lost on passage, one disappeared (*X5*), one (*X10*) abandoned the operation after a series of mechanical difficulties and two (*X6* and *X7*) successfully laid their side cargoes underneath the German battleship's hull. It is not clear how many of the four charges exploded. Post-war hydrographic surveys of the area failed to find any of the charges or even traces of splinters, so it must be presumed that all detonated simultaneously. The damage suffered by *Tirpitz* was extensive. Although her hull remained intact there was considerable shock damage in the machinery spaces. All turbine feet, propeller shaft plummer and thrust blocks and auxiliary machinery bearers were cracked and distorted. The port turbine casing and condenser casing were fractured. The propellers could not be turned and the port rudder was inoperable due to the steering compartment having flooded through a stern gland. The four 38cm turrets had jumped off their roller paths but B and D turrets were quickly repaired. All the optical rangefinders except those in B turret and the foretop were rendered useless. Three of the four flak directors were out of

action and the aircraft catapult was unserviceable. One seaman was killed and forty more injured. Operations 'Guidance', 'Heckle' and 'Struggle' were similar anti-shipping operations. In 'Guidance' and 'Heckle' the target was a floating dock at Bergen which was increasingly being used for U-boat repair work. *X24*'s first attack in April 1944 was a failure because the explosive charges were laid under the merchant ship *Barenfels* instead of the dock itself. But the validity of the operation had been proved. An *X-Craft* had successfully penetrated an enemy harbour and returned unscathed, leaving the enemy none the wiser as to cause of an explosion which had sunk a merchant ship and demolished a good portion of the wharf! The operation was successfully repeated in 'Heckle' later that year – the dock along with two merchant ships lying alongside it was sunk. Likewise Operation 'Struggle' was an operation against the Japanese cruisers *Takao* and *Myoko* which, though no longer seaworthy, were in a position to dominate the landward approaches to Singapore with their ten 8in guns. *Myoko* was not attacked because *XE1* was delayed on her run-in by tides, so both *X-Craft* laid their charges under *Takao*. Unfortunately the main charge laid by *XE3* did not explode but a number of the limpet mines did. A hole 7m x 3m wide was blown in *Takao*'s hull to starboard and parallel with the keel between frames 113 and 116 and there was some flooding of compartments below the lower deck level. There was considerable shock damage including distorting the roller paths for her main armament gun turrets and damaging sensitive fire-control instruments. Unfortunately, the cruiser sank in shallow water on an even keel and her upper deck remained above the water.

The other *X-Craft* operations represented a new departure for midget submarines and are an indicator of the sort of operations such craft might perform today. 'Postage Able' was the use of an *X-Craft* to land hydrographic experts on French soil to gather data which could not be obtained by any other means. 'Gambit' was the pre-positioning of two *X-Craft* to act as navigational beacons for the first wave of landing craft heading for the beaches on the morning of 6 June 1944. The telephone cable cutting operations in the Far East remain the most significant. These operations greatly disrupted Japanese communications at a critical time in the war and forced them to go over to using radio, with all the benefits for the Allied side that that implied. Space precludes a discussion of the intelligence 'gain' from these operations but when considering that at the time the cables were cut, the Allies were planning the final invasion of Japan, Operation 'Coronet', and any intelligence about the plans and intentions of the Japanese command was of value. The planners or the *XE-Craft* crews were not to know that the atomic bombs would render their work unnecessary. In this sense these operations could be said to be strategic in nature.

The German *Seehund*

Genesis of the design

On the whole, German midget submarine designs owed more to desperation rather than good naval design practice. There was, however, one German design which was a cut above the rest and which, had it not been for the vast array of countermeasures deployed against them, might have made some impact on the course of the war. This craft was the *Seehund* or Type 127 submarine. This was a two-man craft armed with two torpedoes and capable of extended operations.

The origin of the *Seehund* lay in the recovery of the remains of *X6* and *X7* from the depths of Kaafjord. Subsequently the *Hauptamt Kriegschiffbau*[22] produced a design for a two-man midget submarine designated Type XXVIIA, also known as *Hecht* ('Pike'). Like the *X-Craft*, *Hecht* was designed to carry mines to be laid beneath the hulls of enemy ships, but it was substantially smaller and differed from its British counterpart in a number of significant ways. To begin with, *Hecht*'s designers saw no need for a dual diesel/electric motor propulsion system. It was envisaged that *Hecht* would operate submerged all the time and therefore was no need for a diesel engine. The powerplant consisted of an 8 MAL 210 battery based on five 17T torpedo troughs driving a 12hp AEG torpedo engine. Even so *Hecht*'s endurance was a paltry 69nm at 4kts.

Since the craft would have to pass through nets and other obstructions she was not originally fitted with hydroplanes or stabilising fins. Instead adjustable weights on spindles were fitted inside the boat. This method proved completely ineffective since the weights could not be moved quickly enough in an emergency to affect the trim of the boat and hydroplanes and stabilising fins had to be fitted subsequently. Even so, submerged control was very poor. Since *Hecht* would be operating dived, she was not fitted with ballast tanks, and two compensating tanks gave the craft sufficient buoyancy to lie awash on the surface.

Although *Hecht* was designed to carry an explosive charge, Donitz insisted that a torpedo be fitted so that attacks could be mounted on shipping in coastal waters. *Hecht*'s lack of buoyancy meant that only torpedoes without negative buoyancy could be used and these were of relatively short range. Accordingly *Hecht* was fitted for both mine and torpedo carrying. If a torpedo was carried then a further three battery troughs could be fitted. Externally *Hecht* resembled a British *Welman*. In the nose of the craft was the detachable mine. In the forward section was the battery and a gyro compass. *Hecht* was the first German midget submarine to be fitted with a gyro compass which was deemed essential for navigation if the craft were to be spending so much time submerged. Behind the battery was the control compartment with seats for the two-man crew, another new departure for the Germans. The two men could offer each other mutual support and share the watchkeeping/routine maintenance load. The crew sat in seats arranged fore and aft on the centre line with the engineer sitting forward and the commander aft. The latter was provided with a simple periscope and a plexiglass dome for navigation purposes. Further aft was the electric motor.

On 18 January 1944 Donitz discussed the new design with Hitler who expressed his approval for these new craft. On 9 March contracts were placed with Germaniawerft for the construction of a prototype, followed by another for fifty-two boats on 28 March. The fifty-three boats were built between May and August 1944: none saw active service but all were employed in the training role for *Seehund* crews. At the same time as the orders were being placed, numerous variations on the *Hecht* were under consideration. The first was the Type XXVIIB which had increased range, an armament of two torpedoes and dual diesel/electric propulsion. The initial design was complete by the end of June 1944 and showed a craft which strongly resembled *Hecht* in many ways but which was fitted with a ship-shaped casing for better seakeeping while on the surface, and saddle tanks. More room had been created inside the craft by placing the battery troughs in the keel while the two torpedoes were slung externally in recesses in the hull. A

22hp diesel was fitted for surface travel and it was estimated that this would provide a surface speed of 5.5kts, while a 25hp electric motor gave a submerged speed of 6.9kts.

A variant of the Type XXVIIB was the *Klein U-boot K* which differed only in that it was powered by a closed-cycle engine. The proposal came from Chief Naval Construction Adviser Kurzak who was the *Kriegsmarine*'s representative for closed-cycle propulsion at Germaniawerft. The boat was powered by a 95hp diesel engine commonly used in the *Kriegsmarine*'s small boats and which therefore available in quantity. The engine ran off oxygen, 1250 litres of which were stored in the boat's keel at four times atmospheric pressure. It was anticipated that the boat would have a maximum submerged speed of 11-12kts and a range of 70 miles at that speed. For long-range travel, the boat would have a range of 150 miles at 7kts. Kurzak presented his design at a meeting chaired by Vice-Admiral Heye on 21 May 1944 and was requested to develop a closed-cycle engine appropriate for such a submarine.

Construction and design

Kurzak's proposal had a considerable influence on the final variant of the Type XXVII. This finally emerged as the Type XXVIIB5, better known as the *Seehund* ('Seal') or Type 127. *Seehund* had a boat-shaped hull with a small raised platform amidships containing the air intake mast, the magnetic compass, the 10m periscope and a glass dome for observation purposes The dome was built to withstand pressures down a depth of 45m. The casing contained the ballast tanks and a free-flooding compartment forward. Inside the pressure hull, the layout resembled that of the *Hecht*. In the forward part were four of the seven Mal 210 battery troughs, the other four stowed in the keel. In the centre of the craft was the control compartment with seats for the two operators. The engineer handled the controls and fired the torpedoes on the word of the commander. During the attack the boat was kept at periscope depth and 'talked' onto the target by the commander. The fixed 10m periscope was of excellent design and incorporated lenses which

The *Seehund* or Type XXVII U-boat was the most successful of the all the German midget designs. This photograph shows the craft in series production in the *Konrad* bunker at the Kiel yard of Deutsche Werke in 1945. (US Navy)

Page opposite
Top: A good view of one of the early *Seehunde* being lowered into the water at Neustadt. This boat, possibly *U5049*, is shown fully armed. (K Mattes)

Bottom: Korvettenkapitan (Ing.) Ehrhardt gives *Grossadmiral* Dönitz a tour over one of the first *Seehunde*. Dönitz is seen lowering himself gingerly into the craft. (K Mattes)

allowed the commander to search the skies before surfacing – vital in view of the overwhelming air superiority now possessed by the Allies. The armament of the *Seehund* was the standard two G7e torpedoes slung in recesses under the hull, which meant that the boat had to be removed from the water before loading weapons – a tiresome procedure at the best of times.[23]

In the after part of the boat was the diesel and electric motor. *Seehund* were powered by a 60hp Bussing diesel with a 25hp AEG electric motor for submerged drive. This gave an endurance of 270nm on the surface at 7kts. If exterior fuel tanks were used, the range went up to as much as 500nm – although the crew's efficiency throughout such a long passage would have been doubtful. Submerged endurance was 63nm at 3kts. These figures were rather disappointing and it was apparent that the hull form, particularly when torpedoes were carried, exerted considerable resistance.

The first contract for *Seehund* construction was placed on 30 July 1944. Enthusiasm for this craft was so great that most of the contracts and hull numbers had been allocated before the design was complete. The Ministerial Programme of June 1944 envisaged a total of 1000 Type XXVII boats in service. Germaniawerft and Schichau at Elbing were to build twenty-five and forty-five boats per month respectively. Other centres involved in *Seehund* production were CRD at Monfalcone on the Adriatic and Klockner-Humbolt-Deutz at Ulm. Like so many other schemes in the Third Reich, reality fell far short of expectations. Donitz would not consent to the production of the Type XXIII U-boat being held up for *Seehund* construction, while raw material shortages, labour difficulties, transport problems and conflicting priorities in Germany's crumbling war economy all combined to reduce *Seehund* production. In the event *Seehund* production was concentrated at the *Konrad* bunker under *Germaniawerft* in Kiel which was not longer required for Type XXI or Type XXIII production. A total of 285 units were built and allocated irregular numbers in the range *U-5501* to *U-6442*.

The production schedule for *Seehund* was as follows: September 1944, 3 units; October 1944, 35 units; November 1944, 61 units; December 1944, 70 units; January 1945, 35 units; February 1945, 27 units; March 1945, 46 units and April 1945, 8 units. While the design process was well in hand Chief Naval Construction Adviser Kurzak proposed the incorporation of a closed-cycle power-plant into the design to achieve significant savings in volume and weight. The design was similar to the *Klein U-boot K* described earlier but of slightly larger dimensions. The engine installation, the Daimler Benz OM67/4 of 100hp (with an electric motor for silent creep speed) was selected, and was to be mounted on a common frame which could be simply inserted into the stern section for easy access and secured by a few screws. Significantly, attention was paid to reducing engine noise as much as possible. The common frame was mounted on an elastic bedding using four rubber buffers at the edges of the frame. It was hoped that noise reduction measures would so effective that the silent creep speed electric motor could be dispensed with altogether thus making the power plant extremely simple and light. The closed cycle *Seehund* would have a submerged range of 69nm at 11.5kts or 150nm at 7.25kts.

Development of the closed-cycle *Seehund* was carried out by Ingenioeurburo Gluckauf in Blankenburg and was given the designation Type 227. Contracts for prototypes were awarded to Germaniawerft in Kiel and to Schichau at Elbing and by May 1945 a contract for three operational models (*U-5188* to *U-5190*) had been awarded to Germaniawerft. These models would have used the standard *Seehund* powerplant converted to closed-cycle operation on the grounds that Daimler-Benz engines were not available in any quantity. Tests showed that the Bussing engine could be successfully converted but the war ended before the craft could go into production. Table 18 is a rough comparison between the original Type XXVII, the *Seehund* and the Type 227.

The *Seehund* was the most sophisticated of all the midgets which went into production for the *Kriegsmarine*. From the Allied perspective its small size made it almost impossible for Asdic to get a return off her tiny hull while her very quiet slow speed made her almost impervious to hydrophone detection. As the Commander-in-Chief Portsmouth, Admiral Sir Charles Little, succinctly put it, 'fortunately for us these damn things arrived too late in the war to do any damage'.

Seehund operations

It was December 1944 before the first *Seehund* were despatched to Ijmuiden in the Netherlands. Six were sent by road on 24 December followed by a further eighteen so that by the end of the month there were twenty-four operational *Seehund*. Their operational debut was on New Years Day 1945 when seventeen

Leutnant zur See Ulrich Muller in the conning tower of his *U5329*. Forward of the hatch is the periscope and aft of the hatch opening is the induction mast. Muller has given his conning tower some spotted camouflage in an attempt to render her less conspicuous. However, RAF pilots made spotting the light reflecting off the perspex dome on top of the hatch a favourite activity. (K Mattes).

Table 18: Type XXVII, *Seehund* and Type 227 technical particulars

	XXVII	Seehund	Type 227
DISPLACEMENT:	11.8 tons	14.9 tons	17 tons
LENGTH:	10.4m	11.9m	13.6m
BEAM:	1.7m	1.7m	1.7m
PROPULSION:	1 x12hp ET	1 x 60hp D 1 x 25hp E	1 x 100hp D 1 x 25hp E
FUEL CAPACITY:	N/A	0.5 tons	0.6 tons + 0.72 tons O_2
SPEED:			
Surfaced	N/A	7.7kts	8kts
Dived	6kts	6kts	10.3kts
RANGE:			
Surfaced	N/A	300nm @ 7kts	340nm @ 8kts
Dived	38nm @ 4kts	63nm @ 3kts	71nm @ 10kts
TORPEDOES:	1	2	2
MINES:	1	0	0
CREW:	2	2	2[24]

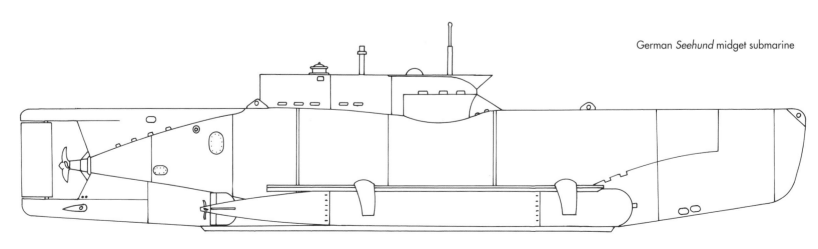

German *Seehund* midget submarine

sailed to attack an Allied convoy off the Kwinte Bank. Seven were later found beached and two returned. Of the remainder the destroyer HMS *Cowdray* and the frigate HMS *Ekins* accounted for one each, another was found abandoned at Domberg while a fourth was found drifting, without a crew, by an MTB. The remaining four disappeared – probably victims of bad weather. The sole gain from the operation was the sinking of the trawler *Hayburn Wyke*. It was not an auspicious start. Bad weather interfered with further operations throughout January 1945, a sortie on 3 January having to be called off together with another on the 6th. However, on 10 January five *Seehund* were despatched to the Kentish coast off Margate. Only one reached the operational area but later returned to base with her torpedoes unfired. Two days later all operations were suspended on account of the weather.

By 20 January reinforcements had brought the number of *Seehund* available back to twenty-six. On 21 January ten *Seehund* were despatched to Ramsgate, the North Foreland and the swept channel off Lowestoft. Of these boats seven returned with defects and two returned having sighted nothing. The story of the third constitutes something of an epic. This boat suffered a compass failure and after attacking a ship in the Thames estuary on 22 January, was driven northwards by the tides until by the 24th she was off Lowestoft where she was attacked by *ML-153* but managed to escape. However, in doing so the craft had drifted even further to the north and was now off Great Yarmouth – unknown to the crew. When they tried to set course to the east and home, the *Seehund* went aground on Scroby Sands where she remained for two and a half days. Eventually the exhausted crew fired distress flares and were taken off by the Trinity House tender *Beacon*. This episode illustrates the considerable fortitude displayed by *Seehund* crews. The fact that the *Seehund* was found so far from home was another fact not lost on the Admiralty. The final *Seehund* sortie in January 1945 was on the 29th when ten boats sailed from Ijmuiden, five for the area off Margate and the remainder for the South Falls area. Only two reached their operational area, the rest returning with mechanical problems.

The *Seehund* faired a little better in February. Operations on the 5th and 10th were unsuccessful but on the 12th five boats were sent out to the North Foreland. On 15 February the 2628-ton Dutch tanker *Liseta* was damaged off the North Foreland while in convoy TAM80. At least two boats were lost in these sorties and several were beached but recovered. A new departure for the *Seehund* was an attempt to use them in the Schedlt estuary in a combined operation with *Linsen* explosive motor boats. On 16 February four *Seehund* sailed for the Scheldt which were followed by fifteen *Linsen* that night. The operation was a failure: of the four *Seehund* two vanished without trace, one beached without having made an attack while the last beached after an abortive attack on a small convoy of landing craft. Since the *Seehund* were no more successful in inland waters than the *Bibers/Molch*, they were redeployed back to open waters. On 20 February three boats sailed for Ramsgate, on the 21st four sailed for the South Falls followed by a fourth on the 23rd. This group had some results: on 22 February *LST-364* was sunk while in convoy TAM87 together with the cable ship *Alert* sunk off Ramsgate on 24 February. All eight returned, one of them surviving an attack from Beaufighter J of 254 Squadron east of Orfordness. A summary of *Seehund* operations in January/February 1945 is given in Table 19.

U5090 returns to Dunkirk just after the surrender of the port in April 1945. Both the crew, LtzS Kunau and Ll Jager, are standing on the casing. (K Mattes)

Table 19: *Seehund* operations January/February 1945

	Sorties	Losses	Results
January	44	10	1 ship sunk (324 tons)
February	33	4	2 ships sunk (3691 tons) 1 ship damaged (2628 tons)

In March 1945 there were a total of twenty-nine *Seehund* sorties of which nine boats failed to return. MTBs sank two, the frigate *Torrington* another, three were claimed by aircraft, one was sunk by HMS *Puffin* and the fate of the other two is unknown. The sinking by *Puffin* was a pyrrhic victory: on 26 March the

Seehund General Arrangement

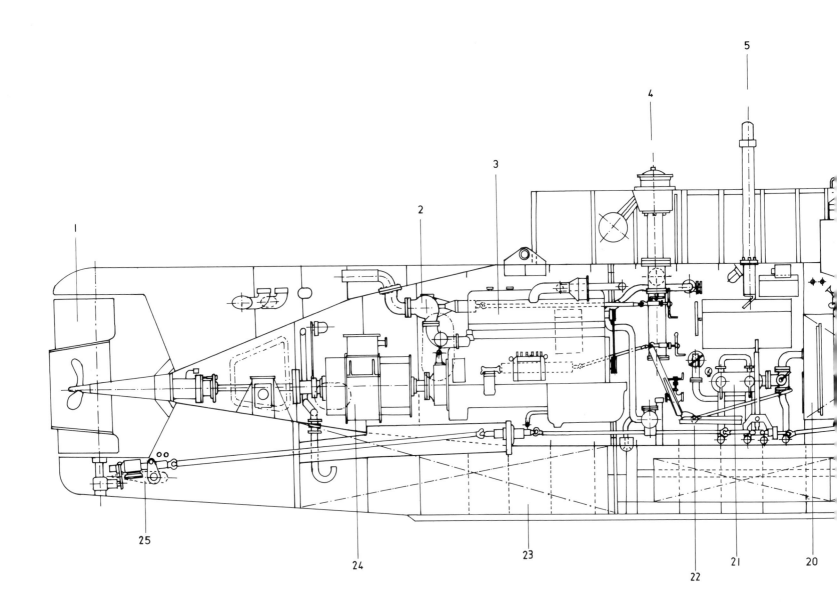

Key

1. Vertical rudder & propeller shroud.
2. Exhaust valve.
3. 6-cylinder diesel engine.
4. Fresh air intake.
5. Projection compass.
6. Hatch.
7. Periscope.
8. Two oxygen bottles.
9. Forward battery compartment.
10. Trimming tank,
11. Forward diving tank.
12. Free flooding space.
13. Three compressed-air bottles.
14. Fuel tank.
15. Automatic steering motor.
16. Combined diving and steering lever.
17. Commander's seat.
18. Midships battery compartment.
19. Fuel settling tank.
20. Compensating tank (port & starboard).
21. Pumping valves.
22. Engineer's seat.
23. Aft diving tank.
24. Electric motor.
25. Hydroplane.

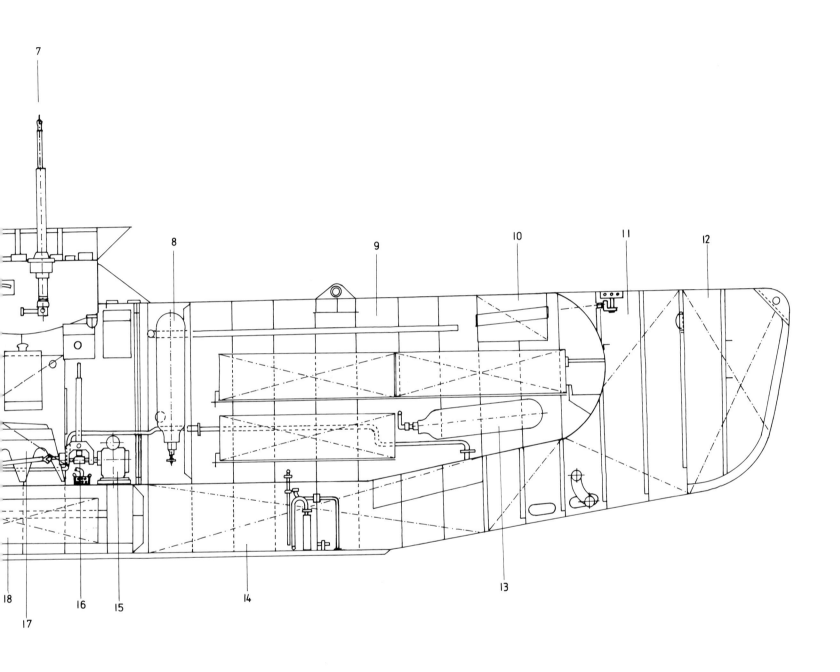

Puffin rammed the *Seehund* off Lowestoft. However, in the collision both the *Seehund*'s torpedoes exploded and *Puffin* was so badly damaged that she was not repaired. But three ships totalling 5267 tons were sunk: the 2878-ton *Tauber Park* on 13 March off Southwold, the 833-ton *Jim* on 30 March south-east of Orfordness and the 1556-ton *Newlands* on the 26th off the North Foreland.

In April the *Seehunde* were the only *K-Verband* craft which could make the journey from Germany to Holland by sea, now that Holland was virtually encircled by Allied armies. Twenty-nine boats remained at Ijmuiden on 8 April of which only 50 per cent were operational. Four more *Seehunde* arrived from Wilhelmshaven on 20 April and fourteen more by 1 May together with two more from Heligoland. In April thirty-six sorties were made for the loss of three craft. In return *Seehund* succeeded in torpedoing the cable ship *Monarch* on 16 April. Nine *Seehund* operated in the Scheldt where they sank the 800-ton US Navy oiler *Y17* on 17 April for the loss of three of their number. From 17 April seventeen boats were ordered to the Dover-Dungeness area where one sank the 7219-ton *Samida* on 19 April and damaged the 7176-ton *Solomon Juneau* on the same day, both ships being in convoy TBC123. However, *ML-102* accounted for one *Seehund*, Beaufighter W of 254 Squadron another, while a third ran ashore east of Calais. On 11 April another *Seehund* attacked Convoy UC63B east of Dungeness and damaged the 8580-ton *Port Wyndham*. This craft may have been the one sunk by *MTB-632* later that day. Yet another was sunk off the Hook of Holland on 12 April and a third on the 13 April by a Barracuda of 810 Naval Air Squadron in the same area. *Seehund* operations ceased on 28 April but they continued to be employed running supplies into Dunkirk. Four boats made this increasingly perilous voyage before the German capitulation.

A summary of *Seehunde* operations shows that there were 142 sorties which resulted in the loss of nine ships totalling 18,451 tons sunk and three ships of 18,354 tons damaged. Against this thirty-five craft were lost. This is a relatively low figure especially considering that twenty of these losses were due to bad weather. Had their crews been better trained and with more experience, a far higher total of shipping would

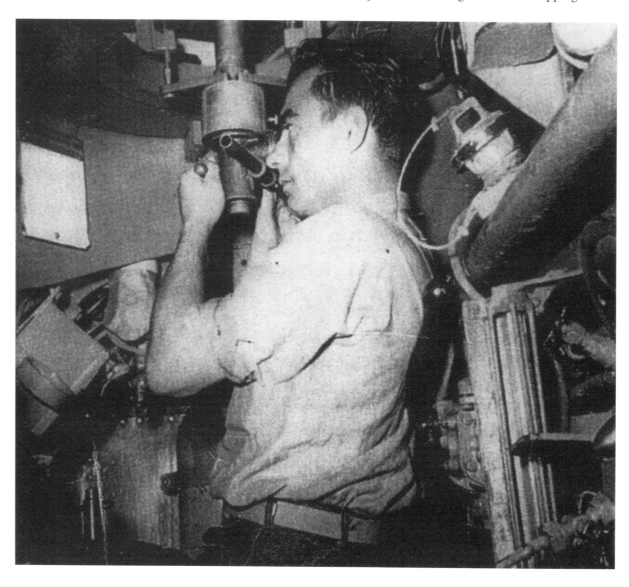

The commander's position in a *Seehund*. Georges Thibaud, the engineer of one of the four craft given to the French, is shown looking through the periscope. (K Mattes)

have been sunk. As one commentator has concluded:

> Fortunately for the Allies, the *Seehund* came too late. A little earlier and Allied ships and landing craft might have suffered disastrously from the attentions of the *Seehund*: anti-submarine defences would have been swamped if large groups had been able to make co-ordinated attacks. It has to be asked whether the situation would be markedly different today.[25]

In retrospect it has to be said that that all the effort expended by the Germans on the *K-Verband* were wasted and never justified in terms of the results achieved. The sheer loss of life in these operations can only be compared with that of the Japanese *Kamikazes*. Any better results could hardly be expected, given the hurried design of the various craft, the hasty training of their operators and the nature of Allied counter-measures. Their sole 'success' (if such a term can be used) could be in the huge numbers of Allied forces deployed to guard against the menace posed by the *K-Verband*. It is estimated that over 500 ships and 1000 aircraft were specifically tasked with hunting German midget craft.[26] Obviously these units and the man-power could have been employed elsewhere. However, playing the part of the 'fleet in being' was no substitute for sinking Allied ships. The following comments on the *Biber* by one perceptive observer are an epitaph for all the *K-Verband* weapons.

> The failure of the *Biber* and, in spite of the courage displayed, of the *K-Force* reflects the failure of the *Kriegsmarine*'s and ultimately, Nazi Germany's ability to wage war successfully at sea. The organisation of the *K-Force* came at a time when the Third Reich, through its flawed strategy was being assailed on three fronts – in Italy, in Russia and from the air – by a combination of the most powerful nations on earth. *K-Force* and the remaining ships of the *Kriegsmarine* failed to stop the invasion of Normandy in June 1944 and the opening of a fourth front. The creation of *K-Force* was a desperate and unsuccessful bid to challenge the Anglo-American invasion fleet . . . the failure of the *Biber* programme and others of Nazi Germany's midget submarine projects reflects the failure of the Third Reich's naval strategy.

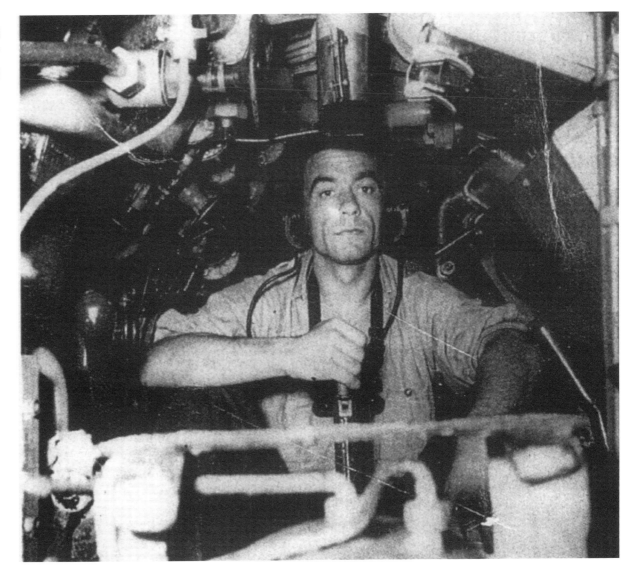

Thibaud is next shown sitting in the engineer's position. Both these internal views show how cramped the interiors were- it is all the more remarkable that *Seehunde* would remain on patrol in foul winter weather for several days. (K Mattes)

The Post-War World

N O REVIEW of submersibles and midget submarines in the Second World War would be complete without a look at postwar developments. During this period 'midgets' have had a chequered history. Of the major powers, Britain, the United States, France and the Soviet Union have all investigated and employed midget submarines since 1945. Cost restraints and the development of other weapons carriers and systems caused all of these countries with the exception of the Soviet Union to dispose of their craft.

Great Britain

In 1945 Britain possessed the largest midget submarine 'fleet' with five *X-20* series craft, six *XT* training craft and ten *XE* craft. The drastic reduction of the Royal Navy in the immediate postwar period saw this fleet reduced to four *XE-Craft*, *XE7*, *XE8*, *XE9* and *XE12*, and they remained in service until 1953 when they were sold for breaking up. During this period they spent most of their time testing harbour defences and in participating in exercises against ships of the Home Fleet. In 1947 *XE7* went across the Atlantic to the United States to show off her capabilities, and her performance was largely responsible for America's belated entry into this field. The four *XEs* had shown themselves so useful that in September 1951 four replacement boats were ordered, known as the *X51* class. These were slightly larger than the *XE* series (and were less manoeuvrable) but in all other significant respects were virtually identical. The major differences were that an improved periscope was fitted and that the night periscope was moved forward to the bow where it could be used to guide the craft

A view of one of the post-war *X51* class, in this case *X51* herself, being hoisted out of the water. In this photograph she is fitted with lockers for carrying limpet mines instead of the single side cargo. The ball-shaped object mounted centrally on the casing is a Type 151 sonar set, used to check that the boat was correctly positioned beneath the target before releasing the side cargo and when coming to the surface. (Royal Navy Submarine Museum 0208A)

through nets. The air induction mast now doubled as a schnorckel when the boat was at periscope depth. A Type 151 sonar set was fitted in a dome on the casing and was used for gauging whether or not it was safe to come up. For the first time these craft were given names: X51 was *Stickleback*, X52 was *Shrimp*, X53 was *Sprat* and X54 was *Minnow*.

The role of the *X51* series remained very much that of the *XEs*–harbour penetration trials and exercises. However, there was one role planned for them which would have propelled these little craft into the realm of strategic forces. The British were already aware of the potential threat posed by Soviet midget submarines. After all, it was known that the Soviets had captured a number of German and Italian vessels of this type. It was to guard against such a threat that the British designed and built the *Ford* class[1] seaward defence vessels which carried a hefty ASW armament and sonar suite for such small ships. Now the British sought to use the same weapon against the Soviets.

In 1954 the Royal Navy conceived the idea that a nuclear weapon could be laid by the *X51s* in the approaches to Soviet naval bases such as Kronstadt in the Baltic and the Kola Inlet. The nuclear weapon was based on the payload of the RAF's Mk.1 'Blue Danube' 10,000lb, 20-kiloton bomb but the following year this was dropped in favour of the smaller 2000lb 'Red Beard' weapon. The weapon was given the intriguing name of 'Cudgel' and could be laid at depths down to 300ft. The timer allowed settings at half-hour intervals from 30 minutes to 12 hours after laying or at 12-hour intervals from 12 hours to 7 days after laying. A small nuclear weapon detonated in the Kola Inlet would destroy the entire base. Such attacks were an attractive form of ASW, the so-called 'attack at source'. This option was particularly attractive in view of the fact that a whole new generation of Soviet submarines like the 'Whiskey', based on the wartime German Type XXI design, threatened to negate more conventional forms of ASW. Eventually the project proved unaffordable because of the shortage of fissile material and 'Cudgel' was cancelled at some time between late 1955 and late 1956.

One chance the *X51s* did have of seeing action was in the 1956 Suez Crisis, when it was proposed that the *X-Craft* should be used to destroy the blockships which Colonel Nasser had placed across the Suez Canal. However, the government of the day refused to sanction the inclusion of the *X-Craft* in the Suez Campaign on the grounds that it was 'too much like real war'.[2] The British *X-Craft* unit was disbanded in 1958, cynics suggested that Flag Officer Submarines had been ordered to cut his 'fleet' by four hulls and disposing of the four *X-51s* was the easiest way of doing that. The reality is more complex: *X-Craft* took considerable risks in their peacetime training which horrified the staff. One *X-Craft* commander commented that:

There may have been another reason for their sudden disappearance. Midget submarine exercises and evaluations tended to be frankly hairy, happily hairy, but hairy none the less. The sort of training they were bound to undertake in order to maintain a realistic wartime efficiency in peacetime was liable to attract the kind of publicity that naval officers concerned with PR have always tried to avoid.[3]

France

Another minor participant in the midget submarine field at this time was France. The French took over four *Seehund* after the war and ran them until 1955. It

An *X-51* class coming alongside a jetty. The photograph shows the much larger induction mast fitted to these craft which could also be used as a schnorckel when the boat was running at periscope depth. (Royal Navy Submarine Museum 0311)

Two of the *Seehunde* ceded to France after the Second World War. The photograph shows No.365 (ex-*U5365*) and No.90 (ex-*U5090*) alongside the jetty at Toulon. (K Mattes)

is doubtful whether the French were serious players. More likely the four *Seehund* were visible reminders of *Gloire*, that France had emerged on the winning side in the Second World War.

The United States of America

It was not until the 1950s that the United States Navy showed an interest in midget submarines. During the Second World War the Americans had shown a brief interest in British Chariots and *X-Craft* but had not undertaken any work of their own in this field. The innate conservatism of the US naval establishment may have been one reason why midget submarines were not given more attention but a more important reason was that the Americans had no need for such craft. The immense *materiel* superiority which the United States enjoyed over Japan meant that they did not have to resort to weapons of subterfuge in order to achieve their aims. It was external stimulus, the threat posed by the Soviet Navy in the Cold War, that pushed the Americans into midget submarine development.

A midget submarine was required for two purposes. Firstly to test harbour defences and indicate means of improving them, and secondly as a means of attack. Midget submarines possessed the potential to attack the Soviet submarine fleet in its base in ports like Severomorsk and Polyarnoe in the Kola Inlet. A Working Party to investigate midget submarine developments was appointed in the spring of 1949 on the orders of Rear-Admiral C B Momsen, the ACNO (Undersea Warfare). The first American proposal was from Commander R H Bass USN on SUBLANT's staff, for a midget submarine which could be built cheaply and in sufficient numbers to lay a barrier in a suitable 'choke-point' such as the Greenland-Iceland-United Kingdom (GIUK) gap. The craft could either be of a 'pursuit' type which could chase after a Soviet submarine crossing the barrier, or an 'ambush' type, one that would quietly lie in wait. After much discussion the American requirements grew into two distinct craft. The first was for an 'attack' midget similar to that proposed by Commander Bass and a craft designed for harbour penetration and equipped with Underwater Demolition Team (UDT) facilities. These were designated the Type I and Type II designs accordingly with priority going to the Type I design.

Table 20: Type 1 & 2 technical particulars

	Type 1	Type 2 (X-1)
LENGTH:	55ft	49ft 7in + 4ft mine section
BEAM:	10ft	7ft
DRAUGHT:	8ft 6in (mean draught)	5ft8 (fwd), 6ft 9in (aft)
DISPLACEMENT:	73/84 tons	31.5/36/3 tons
PROPULSION:	One 180 bhp 6-71 diesel One 110/125shp motor	Closed cycle HTP diesel
SPEED:	7/14kts	
ENDURANCE:	1900nm @ 6kts (surface) 100nm @ 3kts (dived)	
DIVING DEPTH:	225ft.	
ARMAMENT:	Two Mk27 nod 4 torpedoes	XT-20A, 1700lb mine
CREW:	3	4

Use of the radical new tear-drop hull would mean that the Type I would be the first American submarine to be faster submerged than on the surface. The Americans adopted the British practice of towing the midget to the operational area, and of having two crews for each boat, a passage crew and an operational crew. It was estimated that the operational crew could spend 10 days on patrol before being recovered.

The Working Party recommended that four such craft be included in the new construction programme for FY52 and in November 1949 BuShips proposed that six be built (along with six of the Type II) at a total cost of $5.6 million. The formal requirement for the Type I was issued in February 1950 but by April it had been cancelled. However, the design was reborn, as the DSRV–Deep Submergence Rescue Vehicle. The Type I was an innovative, almost exciting design. The prospect of a swarm of such craft being released into a choke point is certainly one of the more interesting 'what if' scenarios of modern naval history. But it must be mentioned that although the craft was technically sound, conditions for the three-man crew would have been extremely tough. Conditions in British X-Craft were abominable and they were

The ill-fated X-1, America's only venture into the midget submarine field. Powered by extremely volatile hydrogen peroxide, she suffered a massive explosion in February 1958 which broke her into three pieces. She was subsequently rebuilt but with conventional propulsion. (Richard Boyle)

engaged in comparatively short operations. A 10-day patrol in some of world's most rugged environments (such as the GIUK gap) would have taxed the crew's endurance to the limit. Operational effectiveness would certainly have been reduced after only a few days.

The cancellation of the Type I left only the Type II in the programme. This was smaller, and closer to the British *X-Craft* in conception. The Type II did not need any of the sophisticated sensors carried by the Type I, merely a sonar comparable to that fitted in the *X-Craft* which was sufficient to detect and evade enemy ships. This design appeared in the FY52 programme as SCB65 and was named *X-1*. The initial design called for a standard diesel-electric propulsion boat which was slightly smaller and slightly slower than the British *X-Craft*. When the design was nearly complete BuShips let the design contract to the Fairchild Engine Division of Fairchild Airplane and Engine Corporation to develop an alternative.

Fairchild proposed an alternative design using a dual-cycle diesel which would function normally on the surface but would burn a mixture of diesel and hydrogen peroxide when the boat was dived. A small motor generator and battery would power the boat's services and provide some measure of control when the boat was being towed submerged. Fairchild submitted their proposal in October 1952. Against the original BuShips design the Fairchild craft offered a higher submerged speed and greater submerged endurance and consequently it was the one selected. *X-1*'s keel was laid on 8 June 1954 and she was launched at Oyster Bay, Long Island, on 7 September 1955. She was provisionally accepted into the US Navy on 7 October 1955.

The hull was originally built in three sections, bow, hull and tail. The bow section, which joined the hull section at frame 7, contained the forward trim tank, main ballast tank, towing cable release gear and the hydrogen peroxide stowage bed and enclosure tank. The hull section, running from frames 7 to 28, contained the control compartment. Two operator seats were located aft with power plant instrumentation on the port side and ship control on the starboard side. Plane and rudder controls were duplicated on both panels so that *X-1* could be controlled from either panel. The hull section also contained No.2 ballast tank which doubled as an exit/re-entry chamber. The capsule containing the power plant was suspended by four dual cantilever mounts located just forward of the after bolting ring. Nearly all the boat's machinery was concentrated in this capsule – the exception being the battery, the ventilation system, the peroxide stowage and delivery system and the fuel system. The tail section contained the main shaft and propeller, after trim tank, No.3 main ballast tank and the stern planes. An addition to the design was a 4ft section inserted in

between the bow and hull sections containing the 1700lb XT-20A mine which was fitted with either a magnetic or a time-delay fuse. The mine rested on support arms above a hatch in the bottom of the craft. The support arms were geared to the hatch opening apparatus, so that when the hatch was opened, the support arms would rotate away and the mine fall free. However, the 'X' designation to the weapon indicates that it was experimental only. There are no records of the delivery system or a dummy of the weapon undergoing trials.

No sooner had *X-1* been completed that than on 24 May 1956 she was placed in a state of restricted availability for correction of faults found by the Board of Inspection and Survey. On 2 December 1957 she was placed 'Out of Service-In Reserve'. While *X-1* was alongside at Portsmouth, New Hampshire, the powerplant exploded. The bow section was blown off and sank some 15ft ahead of the rest of the hull which remained afloat. This was the end of peroxide-diesel propulsion in the US Navy. *X-1* was subsequently rebuilt with a standard diesel-electric power plant and was employed as a trials vehicle in support of various research and development projects. There was no further mention of her role as a fighting warship and with her demise went the American midget submarine programme. Even before the explosion the enthusiasm for midget submarines in the USN had faded, the advent of the nuclear-powered submarine with its almost limitless operational capabilities being far more attractive to the American submarine community.

Throughout the 1960s, 1970s and 1980s the US Navy concentrated on the 'Big Picture', a world war with the Soviet Union which would almost certainly involve the release of nuclear weapons. But the collapse of the USSR and the eruption of many low-intensity conflicts around the world have demanded a more flexible posture by the US Navy, and hence its re-entry into the midget submarine field with the ASDS (Advanced SEAL Delivery System). This is a midget submarine alarmingly like a wartime *X-Craft* but with an almost teardrop-shaped hull and cruciform rudder and hydroplanes. The craft can carry either mines to be laid beneath a target and/or SEAL special forces operatives.

USSR/Russia

The Soviet Union has been the most active naval power in the midget submarine field since 1945. After the Second World War the Soviets inherited a mass of captured German and Italian data and *materiel* to which must be added any information obtained by more nefarious means from Britain and the United States. There are any numbers of reports on the type and number of Soviet midget submarine designs. What is *known* in the new openness following the col-

Table 21: Soviet midget submarine technical particulars

	Losos	*Piranya*	*Triton 1*	*Triton 2*
DESIGNER:	Malachite	Malachite	Malachite	Malachite
BUILDER:	Admiralty	Admiralty	Admiralty	Admiralty
PROJECT NO:	865	?	1083	?
COMPLETED:	1988	?	?	?
DISPLACEMENT:	?/219 tons	?/250 tons	1.6 tons/?	5.7 tons/?
LENGTH:	28m	30.2m	5m	9.5m
BEAM:	4m	?	?	1.9m
DRAUGHT:	3.9m	3.9m	1m	1.6m
DIVING DEPTH:	200m	200m	40m	40m
SPEED (dived) :	6.5kts	6.5kts	6kts	6kts
RANGE (max) :	540nm	1000nm	30nm	?
ENDURANCE:	10 days	10 days	6hrs	12hrs
ARMAMENT:	2 torpedoes	2 torpedoes	N/A	N/A
CREW:	3	4	2	6
FROGMEN:	6	6	N/A	N/A

lapse of the Soviet Union is that four different types of midget submarine were built for the Soviet Navy. Their design particulars are given in Table 21.

Losos and *Piranya* were very similar to the *X-Craft* (but with the addition of a torpedo armament) and could be used for attack operations or for the insertion of *Spetsnaz* special forces or KGB/GRU operatives. The two *Triton* craft were purely for the insertion of special forces. As to means of delivery, the Soviet Union possessed a huge merchant fleet, run under dual naval/civilian control. It is more than reasonable to suppose that the Soviets had created a modern *Olterra* equipped with hatches below the waterline for the exit/re-entry of midget submarines. The large Soviet fleet of trawlers and trawler factory ships would have been particularly suited for this purpose. It has often been noted that some Soviet merchant ships appeared to have holds which were well below the depth of the hull as indicated on the draught marks and that some Soviet Masters preferred to stick to deep-water channels even though the given draught of their vessel allowed them to use a shallower route. It would therefore be reasonable to assume that any Soviet merchant ship loitering around a sensitive area such as the Clyde, the Isle de Longue or Kings Bay, Georgia, could have been doing so 'with intent'. The Soviet Navy also developed two 'India' class rescue submarines. These boats, one which served with the Northern Fleet and the other with the Pacific Fleet, had wells in their after casings to accommodate two Project 1837 and 1837K DSRVs (Deep Submergence Rescue Vehicles). The Russians have twelve (*APS-5, APS-11, APS18-27*) of these 35-ton craft which are able to dive to 2000m and have accommodation for eleven onboard. Ostensibly these submarines are for use in rescue operations, but their military potential is obvious.

The demise of the USSR and re-creation of Russia does not mean that the Russians will abandon their achievements in this field. Historically the Russians have been pioneers in submarine development so their interest in this field is merely the continuance of a long tradition. The possession of midget submarines helps the Russian government fulfil numerous intelligence gathering requirements. There is no reason to believe that as the ex-Soviet forces become leaner, the underwater assault units will be axed – on the contrary. Any drive for quality over quantity in the Russian Navy is likely to maintain, even increase, their position.

The wider world

The post 1945 period has seen a proliferation of midget submarines. Yugoslavia, Croatia, Colombia, Libya, Sweden, North Korea, Iran and Pakistan all possess and operate midget submarines. Italy is a major manufacturer of these craft although the Italian Navy does not itself possess any in their order of battle. They have supplied Colombia and Pakistan and are also believed to have exported some to North Korea. Italian inventiveness in this field has resulted in the appearance of a number of interesting designs. The Italian company *Maritalia* s.p.a has produced a range of three extremely advanced midget submarines at 80, 100 and 120 tons displacement. Britain has also attempted to enter the export field for midget submarines, Vickers producing a design for a boat called *Piranha* which carries two Swimmer Delivery Vehicles or a number of mines. However, this attractive design has failed to excite any interest from potential purchasers. The old Yugoslav Republic was also active in the export field, producing the *Una* midget submarine which is a single-hull boat with a steel pressure hull and a reinforced polyester casing. The boat is electrically driven by two DC motors powered by two storage batteries each containing 129 cells. The boat carries a comprehensive communications and electronics fit including HF transceiver, radio telephone, underwater telephone, gyro compass, electromagnetic log, echo sounder, Atlas Electronik active and passive sonar and a single periscope. The craft has a range of 100nm at 6kts on the surface. Submerged the endurance is 80nm at 8kts and 200nm at 4kts. The normal crew is six but if divers are to be embarked, the crew can be reduced to four so that six divers can be embarked. There is a one man exit/re-entry compartment. Four R1s are carried in forward-facing tubes which could also be used for carrying acoustic/induction bottom laying mines.[4] Six *Una*s were built for the Federal Yugoslav Navy: *Tisa, Una, Soca, Zeta, Kupa* and *Vardar*. The first commissioned in 1985 and the last in 1989. In 1991 *Soca* was transferred to Croatia and has since been substantially modified by the insertion of a midships section containing a diesel generator. The Croatian Navy (*Hrvatska Ratna Mornarica*) is reported to have ordered a 120-ton midget submarine armed with four short torpedo tubes and able to carry four SDVs.

Colombia purchased four 70-ton SX404 midgets from Cosmos of Liverno in the 1970s. Named *Intrepido, Roncador, Quito Sueno* and *Indomable*, these craft are 23m long and carry a cargo of eight divers, two swimmer delivery vehicles and 2 tons of explosive charges. *Roncador* and *Quito Sueno* were deleted in 1981 but the other two are still extant. Just what the Colombian government want these craft for is unclear but presumably they would be useful in one of the festering border disputes which continually bedevil Latin American politics. Pakistan has also purchased midget submarines from Italy. The three Pakistani midgets are of the MG100 design built in Pakistan under the supervision of Cosmos in Liverno. They are a larger version of the SX756 Cosmos design and replaced nine SX404 boats acquired in 1972. They are probably the most capable midget submarines in service anywhere in world and carry a mixed armament of torpedoes, mines and a contingent of swimmers. The two torpedoes are of the AEG SUT wire-guided type and have an active homing capability to a range of 12km at 35kts and a passive homing capability to a range of 28km at 23kts and carry a 250kg warhead. A crew of six is required but eight swimmers can be accommodated along with eight Type 414 limpet mines and three CF2 FX50 SDVs.

On the other side of the world the Democratic Peoples' Republic of North Korea (DPRK) has over sixty midget submarines in service. The DPRK began the programme in the early 1960s at the Yukdaeso-ri shipyard and has more than one type in service as experience gained at sea is incorporated into the production programme. The DPRK is the world's last impenitent communist regime and few details are available for the types and numbers of boats in service. The veil of secrecy on north Korea's midget submarines was lifted in September 1996 when a *Sang-O* midget submarine was discovered aground near Kangnung in South Korea.

Table 22: *Sang-O* technical particulars

DISPLACEMENT:	275/330 tons
LENGTH:	115ft
PROPULSION:	One shaft diesel generator and electric motor.
SPEED:	8/4kts
DIVING DEPTH:	500ft
ENDURANCE:	20 days at sea
ARMAMENT:	Two 2in torpedo tubes
CREW:	14 (up to twelve additional personnel)

The *Sang-O* found at Kangnung was found to have had her torpedo tubes replaced with a bow section containing extra bunks and an exit/re-entry chamber. The South Korean and American investigators found that she carried an amazing quantity of small arms including 197mm and 75mm anti-tank rocket launchers, M-26 hand grenades, AK47 and M.16 assault rifles and other miscellaneous combat gear. Another item of interest was the discovery of over 4000 cigarettes! The *Sang-O* was probably reverse-engineered from a Yugoslav *Una* design with all the problems which that process entails. In particular the submarine's poor speed makes it extremely vulnerable to being driven off course by wind and current.

As well as midget submarines the DPRK also has eight 'Chariot'-like vehicles suitable for swimmer delivery. Eight and a half metres long and credited with a speed of 50kts, these craft make their approach at high speed before ballasting down to launch the swimmers – six can be carried. One such craft was sighted off the South Korean port of Pusan on 20 December 1985.

Just across the Yellow Sea South Korea's neighbour, Taiwan, was another brief member of the midget submarine community. The Taiwanese Navy were, briefly the owners of four Italian built SX404 midgets. These were used exclusively for the insertion of special forces/agents onto mainland China. The four craft were discarded in 1974.

The DPRK has supplied their expertise to Iran in that country's midget submarine programme. The Iranians built their own submarine at Bandar Abbas using German and Japanese Second World War designs as their inspiration. The craft was completed in 1987 but when the trials were unsuccessful, it was taken to Tehran for modification. The Iranian programme was then overtaken by the offer to supply boats from North Korea. The first was delivered in June 1988 and it is reported that a final total of twenty four boats will be delivered. The Iranian boats are reported to be fitted with side cargoes in much the same manner as a wartime *X-Craft*. Likely uses for the Iranian midgets would include attacks on Iraqi offshore oil facilities or the oil facilities of her neighbours across the Persian Gulf. Other areas of potential employment for Iranian midgets would be attacks on western shipping in the Persian Gulf and the infiltration of *agent provocateurs* into Saudi Arabia. Iraq was the final entrant into the midget submarine field. In the summer of 1990 Saddam Hussein's government was in the final stages of negotiations to purchase a midget submarine from *Maritalia*. Fortunately the purchase was blocked at the last moment – Saddam had plans to arm the craft with a nuclear weapon.

New developments

The most exciting and promising developments centre on the field of robotic, unmanned craft which would be rather like homing torpedoes but with a passive/active search capability of their own. The British company Scion has developed *Spur* ('Scion's Patrolling Undersea Robot') while the Americans have investigated Small Mobile Sensor Platforms (SMSPs) deployed from torpedo tubes. In March 1990 the American Defense Advanced Research Projects Agency (DARPA) announced the construction of two prototype Unmanned Undersea Vehicles (UUV). An SSN, USS *Memphis* (SSN-691), has been converted to act as an at-sea test bed for advanced submarine technology including the launch and recovery of UUVs. The UUV is designed as a tactical system which can be deployed from submarines, surface ships or direct from the shore and which can perform a number of functions including mine detection, underwater surveillance, including ASW, and communications. The key to the performance of these functions is advanced electronic systems which include 'artificial intelligence' algorithms that function in the same way as human thought processes. In order to guard against computer failure, the vehicle will employ three fully redundant computers which will employ a 'voting' approach to system management onboard the craft. All three computers must 'agree' on how the craft is run – if only two agree then the craft will continue to operate but less efficiently.

Unmanned vehicles such as SMSPs and UUVs would enable a relatively small number of SSNs to 'control' a large area of ocean through which enemy forces would have to pass. They also offer considerable advantages in the field of mine detection and electronic surveillance. They also have the advantage of being capable of unlimited under-ice operations – a field denied to manned midget submarines.

Conclusions

A number of conclusions can be drawn about midget submarine operations which are extremely relevant today. Firstly, midget submarine operations require thorough and realistic training if they are to be successful. British and Italian operators were well trained and this was reflected in their achievements, while German operators were flung into battle with hardly any training at all and achieved little as a result. However, the ability of the fanatic to score one decisive hit at the cost of his own life cannot be ignored. Secondly, midget submarines can be built quickly, cheaply and in large numbers, and are extremely easy to hide. Thirdly, almost any merchant ship or submarine can be adapted to carry a midget submarine. Fourthly, no defences have ever stopped a midget submarine attack. They have been a hindrance and have deterred an attacker but a small number of the midgets have always got through. Modern bases are virtually defenceless against this form of attack, especially as wartime skills in the field of boom defence have long since disappeared. Faced by the midget threat, simple last-ditch measures such as spilling oil fuel on the surface of the water will render a small periscope useless. The 'Green lobby' would hate it, but against a simple craft dependent on periscope observation of the target, it would be highly effective. Fifthly, one-man operated craft are doomed to failure. A man on his own has too much to do and loses heart. There should be at least two in the crew and for an operation of any duration at least four are required. Lastly the quality of the operators, the 'human resources' is vital. Men best suited to midget submarine operations are those least likely to fit in with the routines of a peacetime navy. It is interesting to note from the British perspective that Australians, New Zealanders and South Africans, whose antipathy to the Naval Discipline Act was legendary, were extremely competent *X-Craft* personnel. The risks implicit in training for midget submarine operations mean that such men have to develop a team spirit unique to their formation – this is what distinguished *Decima Mas* from the rest of the *Regia Marina* and what distinguishes Russian special forces from the run of the mill conscript.

In 1907 the eminent historian Alfred Thayer Mahan wrote in *From Sail to Steam* that:

> It is now accepted with naval and military men who study their profession, that history supplies the raw material from which they are to draw their lessons, and reach their working conclusions. Its teachings are not, indeed, pedantic precedents, but they are the illustrations of living principles.[5]

There is no doubt that midget submarines are still a force to be reckoned with. The development of new technologies will make them even more effective. Midget submarines are a proven and effective weapon of war and it would be unwise for us to forget the achievements of *Decima Mas* and the *X-Craft*.

Sources

Admiralty: Naval Staff History of the Second World War; Battle Summaries Nos. 15 and 16, *Naval Operations off Ceylon 29 March to 10 April 1942* and *Naval Operations at the Capture of Diego Suarez (Operation Ironclad) May 1942* (London 1943)

——, Battle Summary No.29, *The Attack on the Tirpitz by Midget Submarines, 23 September 1943, Operation Source* (London 1948)

——, Battle Summary No.49, *The Campaign in North West Europe June 1944-May 1945* (London 1952)

——, *Submarines Volume 1 – Operations in Home, Northern and Atlantic Waters* (London 1953)

——, *Submarines Volume 2 – Operations in the Mediterranean* (London 1955)

Bagnesco, E, and Rastelli, A, *Sommergibile in Guerra* (Parma 1989)

——, and Spertini, M, *I Mezzi d'Assalto Della Xa Flottiglia MAS* (Parma 1991)

Bekker, C, *K-Men-The Story of the German Frogmen and Midget Submarines* (London 1955)

Borghese, J V, *The Sea Devils* (London 1952)

Brown, D, *Warship Losses of World War Two* (London 1990)

Campbell, J, *Naval Weapons of WW2* (London 1985)

Chaudhury, Rahul R, *Sea Power and Indian Security* (London 1995)

Compton-Hall, Commander P R, *The Underwater War* (London 1982)

——, *Monsters and Midgets* (London 1985)

——, *Submarine vs Submarine* (Newton Abbott 1988)

——, and Moore, Captain J, *Submarine Warfare Today and Tomorrow* (London 1986)

Cruikshank, G, *SOE in the Far East* (Oxford 1983)

Donitz, K, *Memoirs – Ten Years and Twenty Days* (London 1990)

Friedman, N, *US Submarines Since 1945* (Annapolis 1994)

Hashimoto, Mochitsura *Sunk!* (New York 1954)

Holloway, A, From Dartmouth to War – A *Midshipman's Journal* (Buckland Press 1993)

Japanese Maritime Self Defense Agency *Kaigun Zosen Gijutsu Gaiyo* (Tokyo 1973)

——, *Nihon no Kaigun* (Tokyo 1974)

Jenkins, David, *Battle Surface! Japan's Submarine War Against Australia 1942-1944* (Random House, Australia, 1992)

Kemp, Paul, *The T Class Submarine* (London 1990)

——, *Midget Submarines* (London 1990)

——, *Underwater Warriors* (London 1996)

Le Bailly, Vice-Admiral Sir Louis: *The Man Around the Engine* (Kenneth Mason 1990)

Morison, Samuel Eliot, *History of United States Naval Operations in World War II, Vol III, The Rising Sun in the Pacific* (Boston 1948)

O'Neill, Richard, *Suicide Squads* (London 1978)

Padfield, P, Donitz, *The Last Fuhrer* (London 1984)

Polmar, N, and Carpenter, D, *Submarines of the Imperial Japanese Navy* (London 1986)

Polmar, N, and Noot, J, *Submarines of the Russian and Soviet Navies 1718-1990* (Annapolis 1991)

Rastelli, A, *Le Navi del Re* (Milan 1988)

Rohwer, J, *Axis Submarine Successes* (Cambridge 1983)

——, and Hummelchen, G, *Chronology of the War at Sea 1939-1945* (London 1992)

Rossler, E, *The U-boat – The Evolution and Technical History of German Submarines* (London 1981)

Simpson, Rear-Admiral G W G, *Periscope View* (London 1972)

Strutton, B, and Pearson, M, *The Secret Invaders* (London 1958)

Toschi, Elios, Ninth Time Lucky (London 1955)

US Technical Mission to Japan. (The following are among a large number of assessements prepared by British and American personnel who interrogated Japanese officers and examined Japanese equipment.)

  No. 0-01-1 *Ordnance Targets, Japanese Torpedoes and Tubes, Ship and Kaiten Torpedoes* (April 1946)

  No. S-01-6 and 7 *Ship and Related Targets, Characteristics of Japanese Naval Vessels, Supplement 1 and 2* (January 1946)

Waldron, T J, and Gleeson, J, *The Frogmen – The Story of Wartime Underwater Operations* (London 1950)

Warner, Peggy, and Sadao Seno, *The Coffin Boats* (London 1986)

Warren, C E T, and Benson, J, *Above Us the Waves* (London 1953)

Whitley, M J, *German Coastal Forces of WW2* (London 1992)

Ufficio Storico Della Marina Militare *La Marina Italiana Nella Seconda Guerra Mondiale, Vol.II: Navi Miliare Perduti* (5th ed Rome 1975)

——, *La Marina Italiana Nella Seconda Guerra Mondiale, Vol. XIV; I Mezzi D'Assalto* (4th ed Rome 1992)

Williams, J, *They Led the Way – The Fleet Minesweepers at Normandy, June 1944* (J Williams 1994)

Winton, J, *The Forgotten Fleet* (London 1969)

Yutaka Yokota and Harrington, J D, *The Kaiten Weapon* (New York 1962)

Journal Articles

Belke, Cdr Thomas J, 'Incident at Kangnung: North Korea's Ill-fated Submarine Incursion', *The Submarine Review* (April 1997)

Bullen, J, 'The Japanese Long Lance Torpedo and its place in naval history', *Imperial War Museum Review* No.3 (1988)

——-, 'The German *Biber* Submarine', *Imperial War Museum Review* No.4 (1989)

Compton-Hall, Cdr R, 'Minitruders' *The Submarine Review* (October 1988)

——-, Menace of the Midgets, *The Submarine Review* (April 1989)

Fukaya, Hajime, 'Three Japanese Submarine Developments', *United States Naval Institute Proceedings* (August 1952)

Galwey, G V, 'Life in a Midget Submarine', *United States Naval Institute Proceedings* (April 1947)

Itani, J, Lengerer, H and Rehm-Takahara, T, 'Japanese Midget Submarines', *Warship 1993* (1993)

McCandless, Rear-Admiral Bruce, 'Commentary on *Kaiten*–Japan's Human Torpedoes', *US Naval Institute Proceedings* (July 1962)

Torisu, Kennusoke, and Chihaya, Masataka, 'Japanese Submarine Tactics', *United States Naval Institute Proceedings* (February 1961). The July 1962 edition of *Proceedings* contains an interesting commentary on this article.

Walsh, E J, 'DARPA's Unmanned Underwater Vehicle', *The Submarine Review* (April 1990)

Notes

Introduction

1. The officer was TV Gino Birindelli. Many years later Birindelli was told by one of his former captors that the British would have had him killed rather than repatriated. IWM Department of Sound Records: Interview with Admiral Gino Birindelli.

2. Opinion expressed to the author by Admiral Gino Birindelli, 25 May 1994.

3. Convoy PQ-17 was scattered in July 1942 with disastrous results due to faulty intelligence appreciation that the *Tirpitz* and her consorts might be at sea.

4. The Germans had salvaged parts of *X6* and *X7* and had also recovered *Welman 46*.

5. Donitz, K, *My Memoirs-Ten Years and Twenty Days* (London 1990), p369.

6. Ibid, p370.

Human Torpedoes

1. Rosseti, Raffaele, *Contro la Viribus Unitis* (Rome 1925). See also the article in *Marine, Gestern Heute*, No 1 (1978) by Edgar Tomicich.

2. National Maritime Museum: Papers of Admiral Sir Howard Kelly; KEL/4 Autobiographical fragment.

3. Toschi, Elios, *Escape over the Himalayas* (Milan 1957), pp32-33.

4. Borghese, J V, *Sea Devils* (London 1952), p19. Admiral Goiran was the Flag Officer commanding Italy's North Tyrrhenian Sector.

5. Literally 'Slow-Running Torpedo'.

6. The best description of an SLC is in Bagnasco, E, and Spertini, M, *I Mezzi D'Assalto Della Xa Flottiglia MAS, 1940-1945* (Parma 1991), pp129-146. This book is an outstanding account of Italian assault weapons and techniques.

7. Much of the information on the operations launched from *Olterra* comes from a series of papers in the archives at the Royal Navy Submarine Museum and the author is extremely grateful to Commander P R Compton Hall for drawing his attention to them. The papers comprise a complete set of intelligence summaries by Colonel H C Medlam DSO, the Defence Security Officer at Gibraltar, the postwar interrogation of Denegri and others involved and the reports of British agents in Spain. I have referred to this collection as RNSM *Olterra* Papers followed by the appropriate reference.

8. PRO PREM23/3561: Churchill to Ismay, 18 January 1942. Colonel R Jefferis KBE MC an army officer who later served with SOE and pioneered much midget development.

9. Fell, W R, *The Sea Our Shield* (London 1966), p76.

10. See Fisk, R, *In Time of War, Ireland, Ulster and the Price of Neutrality 1939-1945* (London 1985), pp132-4, 135-7, 138-40 for further details of this unusual and little-known operation.

11. The British expert concerned was Captain W O Shelford, the noted submarine escape and salvage expert.

12. Warren, C E T, and Benson, J, *Above Us The Waves – The Story of Midget Submarines and Human Torpedoes* (London 1953), p31.

13. The origins of the name 'Chariot' are unclear. Submariners who carried them into actions referred to them as 'Jeeps' after the rodent-like creature in the *Popeye* cartoon which emitted a series of 'Jeep-Jeep' sounds.

14. Two of the British *Oberon* class SSKs were fitted with a five-man exit/re-entry chamber in the fin.

15. The civil and political head of the Royal Navy, appointed by the Prime Minister with a seat in the Cabinet. Not to be confused with the First *Sea* Lord who is the professional head of the Royal Navy.

16. Simpson, Rear-Admiral G W G, *Periscope View – A Professional Autobiography* (London 1972), p281.

17. Naval Staff History, op cit, p123.

18. Cruikshank, G, *SOE in the Far East* (Oxford 1983), p30.

19. 148 vessels of 152GRT: *Jane's Fighting Ships 1994-95*.

Submersibles

1. Foot, M R D, *Special Operations Executive* (London 1984), pp20-21.

2. This war-winning device consisted of a charge of plastic explosive shaped to resemble cow, horse, sheep or goat dung and fitted with a pressure switch. The rational behind the weapon was that Axis vehicle drivers could not resist driving over a turd. The resulting explosion would, at least, blow up their tires if not themselves.

3. Harvey Bennette to Author, 30 May 1991.

4. Imperial War Museum, Department of Sound Record, Interview with Harvey Bennette, 13244.

5. Bekker, op cit, p19.

6. It was only at the end of 1944 that junior officers from the U-boat arm were allowed to volunteer for the *K-Verband*. The ban on U-boat commanding officers volunteering remained in force.

7. Lt Richard Hale- interview in Williams, J, *They Led the Way – The Fleet Minesweepers at Normandy* (London 1994), p116.

8. Bekker, C, *K-Men: the story of the German Frogmen and Midget Submarines* (London 1955), pp18-19.

9. Cable: a measure of distance at sea, 100 fathoms, 200 yards, 183 metres.

10. Compton-Hall, R, *Monsters and Midgets* (Blandford Press 1985).

11. Admiralty, *Monthly Anti-Submarine Report, March 1945*, p17.

12. Ibid.

13. Ibid.

14. Whitley, M, *German Coastal Forces of World War II* (London 1992), p219.

15. Whitley, op cit, claims three Allied ships sunk in these attacks but this is not borne out by any of the official sources.

16. Bekker, op cit, pp198-199.

17. Torisu, Kennosuke, 'Japanese Submarine Tactics and the Kaiten' in Evans, D C (ed), *The Japanese Navy in World War II In the Words of Former Japanese Naval Officers* (Annapolis 1986), p444.

18. Bullen, Dr J R, 'The Japanese Long Lance Torpedo and its place in naval history', *Imperial War Museum Review* (1988), pp69-79 for details of the Long Lance torpedo.

19. Gardiner, R (ed), *Conway's All the World's Fighting Ships 1922-1946* (London 1980), p217.

20. Torisu, op cit, p446.

21. Kemp, P, 'Only Three Submarine Campaigns?', *The Submarine Review* (July 1990), pp98-99.

22. Bullen, op cit, p71.

23. Torisu, op cit, p446

24. Hashimoto, M, *Sunk! The Story of the Japanese Submarine Fleet, 1942-45* (London 1954), p126

25. McCandless, RADM Bruce, 'Commentary on *Kaiten*- Japan's Human Torpedoes', *US Naval Institute Proceedings* (July 1962), p120.

Midget Submarines

1. See Turrini, A, 'I Sommergibili tascabile della Regia Marina', *Storia Militare* Vol III, No 16, pp34-43, for further details of these craft.

2. *Kaigun Zosen Gijitsu Gaiyo* (Survey of Naval Shipbuilding Technology) Vol 3, p540 indicates that the boat may have been capable of a higher speed, 27.6kts, but this is most unlikely for a 41-ton craft driven by a 600hp electric motor.

3. Commander Takaichi Tanashi to author, 3 March 1994.

4. *Tomozuru* capsized in heavy weather on 12 March 1934 but was brought into port and righted. An investigation found that she was dangerously top-heavy and nearly 60 tons of permanent ballast had to be added.

5. Lieutenant Sekido Yoshimitsu, quoted in *Nihon No Kaigun* No 4 (Tokyo 1978), p28.

6. Itani, Lengerer, and Rehm-Takahara, 'Japanese Midget Submarines – *Ko-Hyoteki* Types A to C', *Warship 1993* (London 1993), p122. This article is without doubt the most authoritative source in English on the *Ko-Hyoteki*.

7. The actual number of *Ko-Hyoteki* built is open to a number of interpretations. Polmar and Carpenter in *Submarines of the Imperial Japanese Navy* state that 62 Type A were built, 1 Type B and 15 Type C, as does Erminio Bagnasco in *Submarines of World War Two*. However, Itani *et al* (op cit. above) state that 52 Type A were built, 1 Type B and 36 Type C. Their justification is that although operational records show that no boat with a number of 85 was used but a photograph showing a boat wearing the pendant number 89 exists.

8. C Type submarines: 2554/3561 tons; 103.80m (pp) 106.95m (wl) 109.30m (oa) x 9.10m x 5.35m; 2-shaft diesels plus electric motors, 12,400bhp/ 200shp, 23.6/8kts; eight 21in TT, one 5.5-in 40 cal, two 25mm AA; 101 officers and men. Five units in class, *I-16, I-18, I-20, I-22, I-24*.

9. This and many following details of *X-Craft* construction are taken from *War History and War Experience, 1939-1945: Technical Staff Monograph on X-Craft.* TS copy extant in the Naval Historical Branch at the Ministry of Defence.

10. Commander C H Varley DSC M.I.Mech.E RN: 1890-1949; Obituary in *The Times* 4 September 1949.

11. An acronym formed from the surnames of the two designers: *Var*ley and *Bel*l.

12. See Kemp, P J, *The T Class Submarine* (London 1990), pp14-15, for a discussion of Vickers' problems in this respect.

13. Papers of Commander H P Westmacott DSO DSC RN, Department of Documents, Imperial War Museum, 95/5/1.

14. *War History and War Experience, 1939-1945: Technical Staff Monograph on X-Craft*, op. cit.

15. *War History and War Experience, 1939-1945: Technical Staff Monograph on X-Craft*, op. cit., p6.

16. A disgusting phenomenon unique to the British submarine service and caused by the improper operation of the WC's flushing system so that the closet becomes open to the sea with the result that one's 'deposit' is propelled out of the bowl and across the compartment at great speed, to the accompaniment of cheers from unsympathetic messmates.

17. Papers of Commander H P Westmacott DSO, DSC* RN, Imperial War Museum, Department of Documents, 95/5/1.

18. *War History and War Experience, 1939-1945: Technical Staff Monograph on X-Craft*, op. cit.; para 76.

19. Cdr R P Raikes RN to author, 10 July 1989.

20. Compton-Hall, Commander P R, *The Underwater War* (London 1983), pp136-37.

21. Papers of Commander H P Westmacott DSO, DSC* RN, Imperial War Museum, Department of Documents, 95/5/1.

22. Head Office for Warship Construction, otherwise known as K-office.

23. The Type XXXII U-boat was a projected development of the *Seehund* in which the torpedoes would have been mounted on top of the hull, thus making loading possible under any circumstances.

24. Bundesarchiv Potsdam: *Hauptangaben Klein U-boote*, Stand 25.7.44, Potsdam WO4-12359.

25. Compton-Hall, Richard, *Monster and Midgets* (London 1985), p144.

26. BR1738 *Preliminary Narrative of the War at Sea;* makes the scale of the effort clear.

The Post-War World

1. *Ford* class seaward defence boats. Displacement 120 tons; dimensions 110' x 20' x 5'; machinery, 3 shafts, 2 12 cyl Paxman diesels plus one Foden, 1100/100bhp=18 knots; armament, one 40/40 Bofors, 2DCT; Type 978 radar & Type 144 sonar; complement, 19 officers & men.

2. Commander R Compton-Hall to Author, 25 February 1995.

3. Ibid.

4. Particulars of the *Una* and other Yugoslav midgets supplied by the Federal Directorate of Supply and Procurement, Belgrade.

5. Mahan, A T, *From Sail to Steam* (London 1907), p159.

Index